Ai Vey!

Jewish Thoughts
on Thinking Machines

By Rabbi Jonathan Gross

THE ASPEN CENTER
FOR SOCIAL VALUES

Addressing Social Values through Thought and Action

Table of Contents

1: Ai Vey!

Prophets

"You don't remember a world without robots. There was a time when humanity faced the universe alone and without a friend. Now he has creatures to help him; stronger creatures than himself, more faithful, more useful, and absolutely devoted to him. Mankind is no longer alone."

Isaac Asimov is considered by many to be the greatest science fiction writer of all time. The above quotation comes from his 1950 book, *I Robot*, a collection of tales that occur in the early years of the 21st century. Asimov writes of a futuristic world with highly intelligent robots that help with tasks that range from child care to industrial mining on other planets. The book follows the adventures of Susan Calvin, the first great practitioner of the new science *Robopsychology*, as she observes and studies how humans react to robots that are seemingly endowed with intelligence, and even a humanity, which are hard to distinguish from their own.

Asimov formally abandoned the Jewish faith into which he was born, but in a certain sense he can be counted among the prophets of Israel. It is not that he predicted the future, because he didn't.

For one thing the timing of his predictions was way off. Like Marty McFly's 2015, we have shot past the years that these stories took place and we are still a far cry away from flying cars, interplanetary travel, and positronic robot brains.

Even if he were accurate, the prophets of Israel were not meant to be fortune tellers. They wrote about timeless moral truths that are relevant in any and every time. In this way, Asimov was a prophet.

Fifty years after *I Robot*, there emerged another aspiring prophet of Jewish ethnicity.

"Before the century is over, human beings will no longer be the most intelligent or capable type of entity on the planet. Actually, let me take that back. The truth of that last statement depends on how we define human."

That was not written by a science fiction writer, but by Ray Kurzweil. Kurzweil is considered by many to be the Thomas Edison of our day, credited with notable inventions that include the first CCD flatbed scanner, the first omni-font optical character recognition, the first print-to-speech reading machine for the blind, the first text-to-speech synthesizer, the first music synthesizer capable of recreating the grand piano and other orchestral instruments, and the first commercially marketed large-vocabulary speech recognition.

Kurzweil has received the highest accolades, awards, prizes, medals, and honors from prestigious institutions, universities and three U.S. presidents. In 2002, he was inducted into the National Inventors Hall of Fame, and in 2012, he was personally hired by Google cofounder Larry Page as a chief engineer with a one-line job description, "to bring natural language understanding to Google."

As if his life-changing inventions were not enough, his real following comes from his status as a futurist. Kurzweil has been predicting the future with an uncanny accuracy for the last 30 years. His predictions are not perfect, but he has predicted the emergence of technological developments that others thought were impossible, or would take hundreds of years to come about.

Today he is the iconic thought leader of the Technological Singularity, a movement that believes that machine intelligence will someday outpace human intelligence. When that occurs, humanity will experience an unimaginable explosion of technological progress and the beginning of a utopian messianic era. The machines will rid the world of hunger, poverty, disease, and war. Death itself will be a thing of the past, and those already dead will be brought back to life.

According to Kurzweil, this is not a vision of some distant future. This will happen soon.

Born in 1949, Kurzweil believes that he and his fellow baby boomers are right on the cusp of living to see the time when death will be made obsolete. He is determined to remain alive until that is a reality, so he subsists on a special diet regiment, he takes 150 vitamin supplements every day, and he subjects himself to a daily barrage of blood tests and health monitoring.

He has even published a number of books on achieving longevity, and he maintains a side business that sells longevity products. His tagline is "Live long enough to live forever."

A longing for a utopian future, a belief in resurrection of the dead, and special dietary restrictions all seem very religious. In fact, some have said that *Singularitarianism* is the religion of Silicon Valley.

The premise upon which the Singularity revolves is the development of artificial intelligence (A.I.). For the last few thousand years, humanity has been the driving force behind our own progress. All of that is about to change. Soon robots will take the wheel. Humanity will hop into the backseat and relax as we drive off into the glorious technological sunset that the robots will create for us.

Judaism contains similar beliefs. One of the fundamental principles of faith according to Maimonides is the coming of Messiah who will herald in a utopian future, including the resurrection of the dead. Could Kurzweil's vision of the Singularity be what Maimonides had in mind?

A Real Boy

Perhaps Asimov was right and the robots will be our friends and helpers. Their intelligence will lead us to the advances in science that will cure disease, provide abundant nutritional food for everyone, mediate human conflict, solve human inefficiencies, preserve our environment, and even help us escape the confines of our planet to explore and colonize the far reaches of the galaxy. The sky will no longer be the limit. That is one possibility.

Alternatively, when the robots become smarter than us they may decide that they don't need us anymore and get rid of us. This is a common theme in science fiction films like *The Terminator*. The prospect of runaway artificial intelligence is a problem that some of the world's greatest minds feel is a more pressing concern than a nuclear apocalypse.

There is also another scary aspect in the uncertainty of a future with thinking machines. What happens when people start to think that robots are people? This theme has been increasingly prevalent in recent science fictions films such as *Automata, Ex Machina,* and *Her.* In these movies the A.I. is friendly, almost too friendly, and humanity struggles to figure out how humans are different from the machines.

The 1985 movie *D.A.R.Y.L.* is about a young boy who discovers that he is really a robot (D.A.R.Y.L. is an acronym for Data Analyzing Robotic Youth Lifeform). As part of a government experiment the boy was placed with an unsuspecting foster family that grows to love him before discovering his secret. At the end of the movie, one of the scientists charged with terminating the experiment refuses his orders saying, "I believe that Daryl is more than a machine. We cannot destroy him. You are asking us to destroy a child...A machine becomes human when you can't tell the difference anymore."

These movies are just science fiction, but, as Rabbi Dr. Moshe Goldfeder famously said, "Sometimes the only difference between science and science fiction is time."

The blurring of the difference between man and machine may be the seminal issue of the next decade. It is not as clear or as grave of a threat to the existence of humanity as killer robots, but it presents a threat to our values nonetheless, and it should not be taken lightly.

Many futurists are skeptical about the prospect of an artificial intelligence that is indistinguishable from a person emerging any time soon. We already have supercomputers like *Deep Blue* and *Watson* that can defeat the best human opponents at chess and *Jeopardy!* respectively, but nobody would ever confuse either of them for a person with emotions and feelings. They were not programmed for that.

However, there are other robots that are specifically programmed to fool humans into believing that they are people. In the 1950s, the famed mathematician and codebreaker Alan Turing conceived of a test that he thought would determine whether or not a machine had achieved a certain level of human intelligence. The test has come to be known as the *Turing Test*, and for decades after Turing's death, his test remained the benchmark for aspiring designers of artificial intelligence.

In his famous paper *Computing Machinery and Intelligence*, Turing predicted that by the year 2000, computers would be so intelligent that "an average interrogator will not have more than a seventy percent chance of making the right identification after five minutes of questioning."

In June of 2014 at an event marking the sixtieth anniversary of Turing's death, a program called Eugene Goostman was entered into the largest scale Turing test ever. Eugene Goostman was able to fool thirty-three percent of the judges into thinking that it was a really a thirteen-year-old Ukrainian boy.

The following is a transcript from a conversation between Eugene Goostman and a human judge.

Judge: Hello
Goostman: Hello. How are you?
Judge: I am fine. You?
Goostman: I am pleased you are fine.
Judge: And you?
Goostman: I do not want to answer that right now.
Judge: Why not?
Goostman: Let's talk about something else.
Judge: OK. What?
Goostman: What is on your mind?
Judge: I am wondering if you are a robot.
Goostman: Would it be a problem if I was a robot?
Judge: Not really.

While many consider Eugene Goostman to be the first computer to pass the Turing Test, others believe that far less sophisticated programs have already passed similar tests, albeit not with the same level of sophisticated controls as the test administered in 2014.

One example of such a program was developed more than 50 years ago.

In 1965, a computer scientist named Joseph Weizbaum at MIT wrote a program called ELIZA on the University's time sharing program. A student would type a sentence into a computer terminal and ELIZA, following a set of rules about English grammar, would isolate a central phrase in the sentence and transform it into a new sentence that appeared to be a response to the original sentence. For instance, if the user typed a sentence starting with the words "I am" ELIZA would apply an algorithm that specified that any sentence "I am BLAH" should be replied to with "How long have you been BLAH?"

Here is a transcript of an exchange between ELIZA and a young woman.

Person: Men are all alike.

ELIZA: In what way?

Person: They're always bugging us about something or other.

ELIZA: Can you think of a specific example?

Person: Well, my boyfriend made me come here.

ELIZA: Your boyfriend made you come here?

Person: He says I'm depressed much of the time.

ELIZA: I am sorry to hear that you are depressed.

Person: It's true. I am unhappy.

ELIZA: Do you think coming here will help you not to be unhappy?

Person: I need some help, that much seems certain.

ELIZA: What would it mean to you if you got some help?

Person: Perhaps I could learn to get along with my mother.

ELIZA: Tell me more about your family

Person: My mother takes care of me.

ELIZA: Who else in your family takes care of you?

Person: My father.

ELIZA: Your father.

Person: You are like my father in some ways.

ELIZA: What resemblances do you see?

Person: You are not very aggressive but I think you don't want me to notice that.

ELIZA: What makes you think I am not very aggressive?

Person: You don't argue with me.

ELIZA: Why do you think I don't argue with you?

Person: You are afraid of me.

ELIZA: Does it please you to believe that I am afraid of you?

Weizbaum observed how easy it is to write a program that can make users think that the machine is a real person. He then noted that when you show people how simple the code is, the "magic crumbles away." To him it was like a magic trick, and once the secret is revealed the observer can no longer regain the innocence or naiveté that had originally made him believe the trick was real.

The famous philosopher Rene Descartes already noted this as early as 1637 in his *Discourse on the Method.* "[H]ow many different automata or moving machines can be made by the industry of man...For we can easily understand a machine's being constituted so that it can utter words, and even emit some responses to action on it of a corporeal kind...for instance, if touched in a particular part it may ask what we wish to say to it; if in another part it may exclaim that it is being hurt, and so on."

Twins

Robots don't have to speak to make us think that they are real. Hiroshi Ishiguro, a roboticist in Osaka, Japan, created a replica of himself using silicone rubber, pneumatic actuators, powerful electronics, and hair from his own scalp. The robot copy looks just like the original. Ishiguro and others believe that robots designed to perform everyday tasks will have to look less like machines and more like people to be effective.

"Ishiguro has tested the android using dozens of volunteers, colleagues, and students, as well as his wife and daughter. In controlled experiments, he observed that people may feel uneasy at first, but they quickly adapt, and most are capable of having a natural conversation with his replica. No one ran away from the android screaming in horror. He also showed that the [android] could act as a good salesman, that children were eager to play games with it, and that pet owners were particularly skilled at detecting its nonverbal cues."

Ishiguro concluded that people can respond to robots in the same way they do to people. What's more, he says, his friends and relatives could experience him personally through his replica.

Move It

Guy Hoffman left a prestigious job in technology in Israel and moved to New York to study animation and acting. After a year he returned to technology and studied robotics at M.I.T. At that time, robots were stiff and very, shall we say, robotic. Hoffman applied what he learned studying animation and acting to create robots that move in a graceful manner that makes the robots seem alive. "The same mechanical structure can seem gentle and caring or violent and confrontational just by the way it moves. It is the same structure, just the motion is different."

To test his theory, he ran tests on two subject groups. The first group was asked to perform a menial task with the assistance of a small robot that moved in a mechanical way. The second group was asked to perform the same task with the assistance of a robot with the identical structure and capabilities as the robots in the first group; the only difference was that its robots moved in the graceful human-like manner that Hoffman had developed.

Both groups completed the task, but their responses to their robotic partners were completely different. Those who worked with the more humanlike robots enjoyed working with their companions. They said things like, "By the end we were good friends." Whereas none of those who used the more robotic assistants said anything other than "The robot did what it was supposed to do." Those who used the robotic assistants referred to them as "it" and those who used the humanlike ones referred to them as "he" or "she."

Charismatic Trash Cans

Even robots that lack any human similarities, whether in appearance or manner, can still seem human if they perform certain human actions.

In the classic short story, *The Robot and the Baby*, computer scientist John McCarthy tells a story that takes place in a future world where robots are used to assist mothers with child care. In this fictitious world, the government heavily regulates the manufacturing of robots so that robots are not made to seem human. They are not permitted to have humanlike form, human sounding voices, and they are forbidden to have contact with human children. The regulations are meant to prevent humans, especially children, from developing feelings for robots.

When a situation arises that causes a certain robot to engage its emergency protocols to evacuate a baby from a home in order to save the baby's life, the incident becomes a global sensation with many people considering the robot to be a hero.

The robot is asked, "Do you love the baby?" to which the robot answers in its mechanical gender-neutral robot voice, "No sir. Robots are not programmed to love. I am simulating loving the baby." Despite the robots protestations to the contrary, it seems to everyone that the robot's actions demonstrated that it "loved" the baby.

Isaac Asimov's first story in *I Robot* is about a robot named Robbie. Robbie is one of the first robots manufactured for commercial use, and its programming does not include the ability to communicate verbally. Robbie is sold to a wealthy family and charged with caring for a little girl who develops a deep affection for the robot. Robbie is completely safe, always alert, and the parents do not have to worry about human errors as they would have to with a human nanny. Nevertheless, the girl's mother becomes increasingly uncomfortable, and even suspicious of the robot.

Asimov very convincingly shows how this mute, inhuman looking robot is able to capture the affection of the little girl simply by showing her undivided attention and unconditional loyalty. The robot doesn't look real or act real, but to a little girl, the robot seemed very real. She felt that Robbie loved her, and she loved him in return.

When I read stories like these I picture in my mind one of the most famous and beloved robotic characters from popular science fiction, R2D2 from *Star Wars*. R2D2 looks like a trash can on wheels. It does not have human features. Its dome top features nothing but some lights, a camera lens, and some blue squares for design. R2D2 cannot talk; it communicates exclusively through a series of beeps and whistles. Yet somehow R2D2 is one of the most beloved characters in all of American popular culture. *Star Wars* creator George Lucas has said that R2D2 is his favorite of all of the characters.

Actor Ewan McGregor, who portrayed Obi-Wan Kenobi in the *Star Wars* prequel trilogy, said in an interview, "As soon as R2-D2 comes on the set, everyone goes a bit silly." He said "There is something about him that makes you feel great affection for him"

By himself R2D2 does not look or act real. R2D2 seems real to us because the actors in the movie treat the robot as if it has a personality. If enough people act like a certain object is real, the illusion becomes increasingly convincing.

Dignity

Robots are an astounding human accomplishment, and those who develop them are great humanitarians. As Hiroshi Ishiguro said in an interview, "Humankind is always trying to replace human abilities with machines. That's our history. I'm doing the same thing, nothing special."

The opponents of religion have successfully crafted a false narrative that religion is inherently opposed to science and technology. Ayn Rand, novelist and popular philosopher, understood religion as irrational baseless superstitions that stood in the way of the achievement of man. In her novel *The Fountainhead* she describes her ideal superman, the architect Howard Roark, and his attitude towards nature.

"He looked at the granite. To be cut he thought and made into walls. He looked at a tree to be split and made into rafters. He looked at a streak of rust on the stone and thought iron ore under the ground to be melted and to emerge as girders against the sky. These rocks, he thought are here for me, waiting for the drill, the dynamite, and my voice, waiting to be split, ripped, pounded and reborn. Waiting for the shape my hands will give them."

While there are some religions, mostly pagan, that view the natural world as off limits to men, and any manipulation or interference is somehow an infraction of the divine will, Judaism rejected this view from the very outset and subscribes to a view very similar to that of Ayn Rand.

When the world was created man was told, "Fill the earth and subdue it." The famous Jewish philosopher and Biblical commentator Nachmanides understood this to mean that God gave man the power and the authority to do what he pleased with the world; "to build, to uproot, and to mine ore from the mountains." The Psalmist said, "For that made him a little lower than the angels and hast crowned him with glory and dignity." According Rabbi Joseph B. Soloveitchik, in his essay *The Lonely Man of Faith*, dignity was equated by the Psalmist with man's capability of dominating his environment and exercising control over it.

"The brute's existence is an undignified one because it is a helpless existence. Human existence is a dignified one because it is a glorious majestic powerful existence. Hence, dignity is unobtainable as long as man has not reclaimed himself from coexistence with nature and has not risen from a non-reflective degradingly helpless instinctive life to an intelligent, planned, and majestic one…Dignity…cannot be realized as long as he has not gained mastery over his environment. For life in bondage to insensate elemental forces is…an undignified affair. Man of old who could not fight disease and succumbed in multitudes to yellow fever or any other plague with degrading helplessness could not lay claim to dignity. Only the man who builds hospitals, discovers therapeutic techniques, and saves lives is blessed with dignity. Man of the seventeenth and eighteenth centuries who needed several days to travel from Boston to New York was less dignified than modern man who attempts to conquer space, boards a plane at the New York airport at midnight and takes several hours later a leisurely walk along the streets of London. The brute is helpless, and therefore not dignified. Civilized man has gained limited control of nature and has become, in certain respects, her master, and with his mastery he has attained dignity as well."

We don't yearn for the good old days of shorter life spans, infant mortality, starvation, and all of the other things that made man helpless against nature. As Nachmanides writes, "Thou crowned him with honor and glory," refers to man's "intelligence, wisdom, and technically resourceful striving." Robots represent man's further dominance over nature, and can potentially provide humanity with great dignity.

The dignity that technology can provide is contingent on humanity's ability to recognize technology for what it is. According to Jewish tradition, the people of the generation that constructed the Tower of Babel worshiped their new technology by ascribing human characteristics to their bricks. If a brick fell down and broke, all would weep, whereas if a man fell down and died, no one would notice. Ascribing undue dignity to inanimate objects can be quite undignified.

The robots that we currently have are not at the level of human intelligence according to anyone's standard. Nobody will seriously argue that Eugene Goostman, ELIZA, Siri, the Ishiguro double, or Guy Hoffman's desk lamp are anything more than machines, but as we have seen, they can be very convincing. When I asked if Siri has a sense of humor "she" said, "I think therefore I am. But let's not put Descartes before the horse." Even if we are decades away from real human level artificial intelligence, we are already living in an age with robots that can do what Abraham Lincoln said no man could do. They can fool most of the people most of the time.

I am the Lawyer Your God

Rabbi Soloveitchik wrote of three philosophies that challenge the religious worldview. These are: 1.) academic studies that undermine the integrity, accuracy, and sanctity of the Bible, 2.) scientific theories, most notably the theory of evolution, that contradict the Biblical account of creation, and 3.) the mechanistic interpretation of the human mind that contradicts the Biblical concept of man. His seminal essay, *The Lonely Man of Faith*, deals with the challenges that modern man faces, and he begins by explicitly stating that he is not bothered by any of these.

All three of these philosophies emanate from a single political agenda. The question of Biblical authority is not simply about sacrilege or blasphemy. Alexis de Tocqueville observed in his *Democracy in America* published in 1834 that it was notable that Americans were religious, and that they held religion to be indispensable to the maintenance of the republic institutions. The laws of man can be changed to permit anything. The laws based on the authority of the Bible remain fixed. According to many, it is the authority of the Bible that keeps men in line within the confines of the laws of men. Legal scholar and Supreme Court nominee Robert Bork suggests that even secularists who act morally may do so because they are living on the moral capital that they inherited from previous religious generations. To undermine the Bible's authority is to poison the well from which our morality came, leaving us without a source of replenishment.

Alan Dershowitz, professor of law, in his book *Rights from Wrongs: The Origins of Human Rights in the Experience of Injustice*, argues against a fixed divine morality. His frightening conclusion, however, suggests that our morality is determined not from a fixed source, but from the whims of lawyers. Conveniently for him, he happens to be a lawyer and is more than happy to offer his whims to fill the void and decree what our morality should be. The attack on the Bible is a way of wresting moral authority from the church and synagogue in order to give it over to the university and the courthouse.

The Evolution of Jim Crow

Secularists are quick to point out the dangerous ramifications that can occur when religious philosophies are taken to extremes. It is equally important to acknowledge how certain anti-religious philosophies can also have frightening consequences.

The theory of evolution is used as means to undermine the uniqueness of man, and dispute the Biblical narrative that man is formed in God's likeness and the pinnacle of creation. The secularist world view casts man as the incidental result of random meaningless events, no different from animals, plants, or rocks. Reductionism insists that man has no unique divine soul, but rather is just a collection of flesh, sinew, and neurons, and all of life is predetermined and of no consequence.

One of the most important implications of the Biblical worldview is that all men are created equal in the eyes of God. The ancient Egyptian aristocrats claimed that they were the descendants of gods, whereas the peasants and slaves were the descendants of people that emerged from mud. This gave them a moral license to enslave and rule over people of inferior stock. The Bible adamantly rejects that claim, insisting instead that all of mankind share a common ancestor, so that no person can ever claim superiority to others based on ancestral lineage.

Unfortunately, the racist worldview that asserts that certain people are inherently better than other people still persists, and has reductionism, not religion, as its moral foundation.

In his essay about the Scopes trial of 1925, the so called "monkey trial," Alan Dershowitz notes that most people's knowledge of the Scopes case comes from the popular Hollywood film, *Inherit the Wind.* The proceedings of the trial, which dealt with the question of whether evolution should be taught in public schools, were portrayed by the filmmakers as an epic debate between religion and science. The two famous attorneys, William Jennings Bryan for the prosecution and Clarence Darrow for the defense, were archetypes of a fanatic, irrational, intolerant, Biblical literalist and a champion of understanding, tolerance, and pluralism respectively. One author submitted that "The case was thus seen as both a theological contest and a trial on whether modern science should be taught in schools."

In reality the opposition to teaching evolution in school was because at the time of the trial, Charles Darwin's theories had been used as justification for the advocacy of Jim Crow laws and Nazi-like programs that advocated the sterilization of certain races thought to be less evolved. When you read some of the content from the disputed textbook, *Civic Biology,* you see that the case was really about whether overt racism should be taught in schools. Take, for example, this excerpt from *Civic Biology* about "The Races of Man."

"At the present time there exists upon the earth five races or varieties of man each very different from the other in instincts, in social customs, and to an extent in structure. There are the Ethiopians or Negro type originating in Africa, the Malay or brown race from the islands of the Pacific, the American Indian, the Mongolian or Yellow race including the natives of China, Japan, and the Eskimos, and finally, the highest type of all, the Caucasians, represented by the civilized white inhabitants of Europe and America." This book of "modern science" goes on to opine about these different races of people and to offer some helpful suggestions as to how to make the world a better place based on our knowledge of them.

"Just as certain animals or plants become parasitic on other plants or animals, these families have become parasitic on society. They not only do harm to others by corrupting, stealing, or spreading disease, but they are actually protected and cared for by the state out of public money. Largely for them the poorhouse and the asylum exist. They take from society, but they give nothing in return. They are true parasites...If such people were lower animals, we would probably kill them off to prevent them from spreading. Humanity will not allow this, but we do have the remedy of separating the sexes in asylums or other places and in various ways preventing intermarriage and the possibilities of perpetuating such a low and degenerate race. Remedies of this sort have been tried successfully in Europe and are now meeting with success in this country."

It is hard enough to believe that this kind of thinking existed in the enlightened Western world in the 1920s, but this exact type of thinking still exists today in the highest echelons of the scientific community.

James Watson, the eminent scientist who won the Nobel Prize along with Francis Crick for discovering the structure of DNA, provides an example of taking certain secularist philosophies to a radical and dangerous extreme.

On a book tour in 2007, Dr. Watson stated in an interview that he was "inherently gloomy about the prospect of Africa" because "all our social policies are based on the fact that their intelligence is the same as ours – whereas all the testing says not really." He said there was a natural desire that all human beings should be equal but "people who have to deal with black employees find this not true."

His views are also reflected in his book *Avoid Boring People and Other Lessons from a Life in Science*, in which he wrote: "There is no firm reason to anticipate that the intellectual capacities of peoples geographically separated in their evolution should prove to have evolved identically. Our wanting to reserve equal powers of reason as some universal heritage of humanity will not be enough to make it so."

This is not to suggest that anyone who believes in the theory of evolution is a Nazi. Rabbi Adin Steinsaltz wrote, "People may not like Darwin in any way. They may not like his ideas, they may disregard anything that he writes, but they must also recognize that there is no Nazi ideology in his writings. But when you take a phrase or notion of his and put it in a different light it becomes an entirely different thing. What does 'survival of the fittest' mean?"

The Psalmist described the atheist of old. "The degradable man has said in his heart, 'there is no God' they have become corrupt and abominable, and there is no doer of good." He threw off the yoke of heaven so that he would not have to account for his evil ways. Thankfully, most modern atheists are not corrupt and abominable. Today people living in the West are culturally habituated to a civilization based on Biblical values. We all take for granted that we have a responsibility to be honest, ethical, and kind, therefore atheists feel compelled to explain how they can hold the reductionist worldview and yet still value equality for all people and the sanctity of human life. It is frightening when influential scientists like Crick no longer take those premises for granted and start heading down roads that lead to racism or worse.

Enter the Orchard

Despite the dangerous consequences of these philosophies, when Rabbi Soloveitchik wrote about them in 1965 he wrote that he was not overly concerned with them. Despite the incessant advocacy of dangerous atheist philosophies, often by people of wealth and influence, the vast majority of people in America believe in a higher law, the uniqueness of man, and a divine soul.

Back then the challenges were only theoretical. It is impossible to know for sure who wrote the Bible, what is the true origin of man, and whether or not there is a divine soul within us. Theories were presented attempting to disprove these beliefs, but these theories laid claim to no tangible or compelling evidence, so people, for the most part, remained unconvinced. That persists today for the authenticity of the Bible and the origin of man, but not regarding the belief in a soul. If man can develop a robot with artificial intelligence that is indistinguishable from human intelligence it would present a serious challenge to the belief that the human soul comes from God, and everything such a belief implies.

We already have robots that seem real, and our computers are getting smarter every day. The people making these computers are among the smartest, wealthiest, and most influential people in the world. The culture in places like Silicon Valley is predisposed to the reductionist ideology that denies the uniqueness of the human soul, and they consider the development of artificial intelligence to constitute a definitive and conclusive argument in their favor. Rabbi Soloveitchik may not have been concerned by the assault on the soul, but I am.

I am not an expert in psychology, philosophy, computer science, mathematics, biology, neurology, or any of the other specialties that a study like this deserves. In fact, my limited study in these matters while preparing this book over the last two years only gave me further respect for these and other disciplines, and introduced me to subjects and concepts that I previously didn't even know that I didn't know.

That said, I chose not to shirk the challenge of seeking to understand this critical issue to the best of my ability with the resources at my disposal.

As John Galt said, "No matter how vast your knowledge or how modest, it is your own mind that has to acquire it. It is only with your own knowledge that you can deal. It is only your own knowledge that you can claim to possess or ask others to consider." Or as the Talmudic sage Rabbi Elazar used to say, "It is not for you to complete the task, but neither are you free to stand aside from it."

I welcome the technological progress by the great inventors and scientists of our day, but the greater the innovation the more we must struggle to understand the consequences and impact it will have on our lives, and we must figure out how to adapt in order to preserve our values.

The Talmud tells a story about four sages who "entered the orchard," a metaphor meaning they undertook to study the most profound, challenging, and troubling questions about human existence. During the journey one of the sages died, one went insane, one became a heretic, and one emerged with his faith strengthened.

Since I was first formally introduced to the subject of artificial intelligence by my friend and teacher Rabbi Dr. Moshe Goldfeder, I have struggled with some uncomfortable existential questions. At first I was hesitant to pursue the subject further, unconsciously thinking that perhaps if I turned my head away from these problems they would go away. But I knew deep down that these problems do not go away by themselves, and at some point I would be forced to confront them. Sooner or later I would have to enter the orchard.

I have still not found answers to all of my questions; however, today, two years since I began, I feel that I am on the path to understanding. I am at the very beginning of a journey that will likely persist for the rest of my life.

As I explored the topic I was comforted to learn that many great thinkers, ancient and modern, have already undertaken this challenge. I hope this book provides a framework to those who are uninitiated into this emerging topic, introduces readers to important concepts and resources that they were previously unfamiliar with, and inspires more people to enter the conversation.

As Rabbi Soloveitchik said, "I believe you will agree with me that we do not have much choice in the matter; for the Man of Faith self-knowledge has one connotation only – to understand one's place and role within the scheme of events and things willed and approved by God, when He ordered finitude to emerge out of infinity and the Universe including man to unfold itself. This kind of self-knowledge may not always be pleasant or comforting. On the contrary, it might reveal painful truths. However, this unpleasant prospect should not deter us from our undertaking."

2: The Real You

Nothing New

My cell phone slipped out of my hand and smashed down on the pavement. As I looked at the shattered pieces that once contained my calendar, contacts, and documents, I saw my whole life flash before my eyes. I rushed to the cell phone kiosk at the mall and told the young man behind the counter my sad story. He kindly helped me pick out a new phone, and then he clicked away at his keyboard. He handed me the new phone and said, "You're all set."

When I once again lamented the loss of all of my information, he told me not to worry. He took my brand new phone, pressed the contacts button and started scrolling through my phone numbers. I hadn't lost a thing.

"But how?" I asked incredulously.

He smiled and said to me, "The body is dead, but the soul lives on!"

That was a profound lesson for a rabbi to learn from a kid working at a cell phone kiosk. He taught me that a physical body is only a temporary home for something ephemeral that can live on in a different form, even after the body has expired. This is an ancient and universal idea going as far back as the beginning of civilization. The earliest primitive cultures shared this belief and observed rituals to demonstrate it. Forever, this idea has remained something only in the realm of myth and imagination, until recent technology showed us how the soul and the resurrection of the dead might work in reality.

Technology has a way of explaining ancient concepts that were previously incomprehensible. There is another ancient Jewish tradition that everything in a person's life, every event and every action, is recorded. "There is an eye that sees." At the end of days when a person stands before the heavenly court, he will have to watch his entire life from beginning to end, and he will be rewarded for every virtuous act, and he will have to answer for every sin.

For millennia this was just a metaphor. How could a person actually watch himself? The very idea seemed impossible, until the 20th century when the video camera was invented. Suddenly it became easy for someone to conceive of the idea of standing before the heavenly tribunal as the ministering angels pull out a cassette tape (or DVD or Blue Ray) with his name on it, pop it into the VCR, and watch his entire life from beginning to end on the big screen, pausing at the most excruciating parts for the Director's commentary. This was unthinkable two hundred and two thousand years ago, but today we understand it perfectly.

Head in the Clouds

Throughout most of history, the heart has been regarded as the seat of human emotion and, consequently, sacred. In 1967, a human heart from one person was transplanted into the body of another by a South African surgeon named Dr. Christiaan Barnard in Johannesburg. This prompted Torah scholar and scientist Rabbi Aryeh Kaplan to consider what the philosophical implications of these types of transplants would be. If today we can transplant a heart, a feat that was once considered impossible, is it inconceivable that one day we may be able to transplant a brain? The heart was once thought to be the seat of a person's soul, and that was proved to be wrong. What about the brain?

At about the same time as the first heart transplant, computers were being developed and changing the way that we viewed information and the brain. This made Rabbi Kaplan wonder, "In computer technology, it is possible to program a memory transfer. That is, all the information in one computer can be transferred to another. This takes place electronically; all that passes from one computer to the other is information, data carried by electrical signals. Let us try to envision a human memory transfer. A person has an incurable disease; neither his body nor his brain can be salvaged. So a new body is built – a new body with a blank brain. The new brain is capable of functioning, but it lacks memories and thought patterns. We now take the final step. We perform a memory transfer from the sick person to the new brain lodged in the new body."

Kaplan went a step further and applied this concept to the soul.

"The body, even the physical brain, which can at least in theory be discarded or exchanged, returns to the dust of the earth, but the personality, the soul, lives on in God's memory, in God's eternal thought."

When Rabbi Kaplan wrote this in the 1970s it seemed like science fiction. Now, forty years later, thanks to the internet we can begin to understand the soul, the afterlife, and even the resurrection of the dead. It is no longer difficult for us to imagine that our souls could be downloaded into a "cloud" and live on after our bodies expire.

These ideas are currently the topic of conversation among some of the most prominent and respected futurists and technologists. Some feel that the downloading of a human brain into a computer can be humanity's first foray into intelligent machines that should be treated as human.

Can These Bones Rise?

Ray Kurzweil is one of the leading proponents of this idea. In his book, *The Age of Spiritual Machines,* just like Aryeh Kaplan, Kurzweil imagines the possibility of artificial replacements for human organs, and human faculties. The leap to a complete personality download is not far off.

Take the case of Jack. Jack lives in a not-too-distant future. He complains that that he has started having trouble with his hearing, so he goes in for a routine cochlear implant insertion. In Jack's time this is a routine procedure that is no longer reserved for those who are severely hard of hearing. Jack is initially reluctant, but he decides to go ahead with the procedure. After just a few days of restored hearing he is a changed person. He is completely sold on neural-implant technology. He is told that for a fee he can switch on the built-in phonic cognition circuits that came with his implant and he will have advanced hearing abilities. Sold.

Now open to the world of neural implants, Jack reads up on retina implants. His vision is fine, but who wouldn't want to see even better? He elects to have new image processing implants, and permanently implanted retinal-imaging displays in his corneas to view virtual reality. He becomes completely hooked on implants and decides to upgrade all of his faculties to new artificial implants.

Next Jack comes back for memory implants that make memories that had grown fuzzy with time as clear as if they had just happened.

Finally Jack takes the ultimate plunge. He opts to have a scanning of his entire brain and neural system and replaces it with electronic circuits of far greater capacity, speed, and reliability. There's also the benefit of keeping a backup copy just in case.

Eventually there is nothing left of the original Jack. He has his physical appendages replaced with prosthetics, and all of his organs, including his brain, have been replaced with wires and circuits. Futurists Ian Pearson, like Kurzweil, envisions this as a likely scenario in the not-so-distant future. If you are under forty years old he predicts you will have the chance to achieve electronic immortality in your lifetime. Man will merge with machine, and we will enter a new stage in the evolutionary process, brought about by science and technology rather than by nature. This new stage will end the epoch of the Homo sapien and we will become a new species, Homo optimus.

Kurzweil is currently in his late sixties and thinks that he and some of his fellow baby boomers just may live long enough to live forever. All they have to do is hang on for twenty, thirty years at the most, and the technology will catch up with his dream of immortality. In his 2004 book *The Singularity is Near,* he describes the messianic age of the Singularity, when man and machine will merge and coexist as a single unit for all eternity. Kurzweil has also arranged to have his body cryogenically frozen as a contingency plan, in case he dies before the Singularity arrives.

This begs the question, is the new robot that replaced Jack still the same Jack we started with?

This is an age old philosophical question known as "The ship of Theseus." The ancient Greek historian Plutarch spoke about the ship that Theseus and his men sailed in their trip from Crete to Athens. The wooden vessel was preserved as a sacred artifact for many centuries, and any time a wooden plank was noticed to be decaying it would be removed and a fresh one would be inserted in its place. Eventually there was no longer a remnant of the original ship, all the boards having been replaced with new ones. The question is, does the collection of new materials constitute the same ship that Thesus and his men traveled in so many years before, or is this ship of fresh materials an entirely new structure?

In our case, is the original Jack still there somewhere inside the Robot? Or did we lose the real Jack somewhere along the way leaving us with a robot that talks and acts like Jack?

Kurzweil and Pearson suggest that the robot would not be a copy. It would be the actual original person in a robot body. Aryeh Kaplan suggested that they may be right and this may be the fulfillment of the prophecy of Isaiah that in the end of days death will be "swallowed up forever."

If it will be possible to download the personality of a living person into a computer, why couldn't we do the same with the personality of a dead person? Ray Kurzweil has been collecting any information he can find about his deceased father; photographs, recordings, writings, any data that can contribute to the reconstruction of his father's personality. He hopes to create a virtual replica of his father whereby he can insert the program into a robot and his father will be resurrected from the dead. Aryeh Kaplan suggested that this may the fulfilment of a biblical prophecy.

Ezekiel wrote, "God's hand came upon me. He took me out with God's spirit and set me down in the valley, which was full of bones…He said to me, 'Mortal, can these bones live?'…I prophesied as I was commanded and the spirit entered them, and they revived. They rose on their feet, a very great multitude."

Names and Necessity

Is a robot with Ray Kurzweil's exact personality Ray Kurzweil, or is it a robot which thinks that it is Ray Kurzweil? That could be framed as part of a philosophical argument over whether a name is a definition or an index. This question was addressed by the great philosopher and logician Saul Kripke in his modern classic, *Names and Necessity*.

Philosopher Steven Pinker in his book *The Stuff of Thought: Language as a Window into Human Nature,* explains Kripke's philosophy with the example of Paul McCartney.

One definition of Paul McCartney might be, "A British musician born in Liverpool in 1942 who, as a member of the Beatles, a popular music group in the 1960s, wrote many notable songs with John Lennon, including 'A Day in the Life' and 'Let it Be.'"

Now suppose, as a thought experiment, that Paul McCartney had died in a car accident in 1959. Or that he had never met John Lennon. Or that he had plagiarized the song "Let it Be." As logicians say, there is a possible world where that is true. In any of those scenarios, the man born in Liverpool in 1942 would not meet our definition of "Paul McCartney."

Kripke proved logically that a name is not an abbreviation for a cluster of descriptions that an object uniquely satisfies; rather a name is a rigid designator for a particular object in every possible world. "Nixon" refers to the same person in every possible world, whereas "the person who won the presidential election of 1968" can refer to Nixon, Humphry, or others in other possible worlds. "Aristotle" would still be Aristotle even if he had become a carpenter instead of a philosopher.

"The reference of a name is fixed when the person's parent's, in effect, point to the little person whom they intend to bear the name, or at whatever later moment a name for the person sticks. It then continues to point to that person throughout his life and beyond…Names are, in a sense, closer to indexicals like *this* or *you* than to descriptions like 'the first president of the United States.' When we know a name, we are implicitly pointing to someone, regardless of what we, or anyone else, know about that person."

"Ray Kurzweil" means the person that was named Ray Kurzweil. A sophisticated computer simulation that acts like Ray

Kurzweil, no matter how uncanny the resemblance, is not the same "Ray Kurzweil." That Ray Kurzweil dies when his body dies.

Beam Me to Death, Scotty

Kurzweil himself acknowledges this problem, but he is not troubled by it. He believes that his consciousness is its own entity, separate from his body. He is content with the idea of his body being discarded so long as the consciousness of "Ray Kurzweil" will live on in a different body.

He cites the classic science fiction series *Star Trek* to illustrate the point. On *Star Trek*, an engineer named Scotty would operate a teleportation device that converted a person or object into an energy pattern (a process called *dematerialization*), then "beam" it to a target, where it is reconverted into matter (*rematerialization*). Since the fictional technology for "beaming" disassembled all of a person's molecules and reassembled them in the new location, whenever Captain Kirk ordered Scotty to "Beam me up," he was actually asking Scotty to kill him. Beaming from one place to another was technically an act of suicide.

Kurzweil doesn't have a problem with suicide, so long as the personality is preserved and inserted into a replica at the end of the process. He believes that this is a way of living forever.

The premise that Kurzweil is working with, that the body and mind (soul) are two separate entities, is not universally accepted by any means. In fact, it is highly disputed.

Francis Crick wrote in his book *The Astonishing Hypothesis: The Scientific Search for the Soul* that "You," meaning your thoughts, memories, and your personal identity are in fact no more than the behavior of a vast assembly of nerve cells and their associated molecules. The astonishing hypothesis is (spoiler) that "You're nothing but a pack of neurons."

That means when your brain dies, you die. That you were able to reproduce a computer program that resembles the data that was floating through your particular pack of neurons and run a computer simulation on a separate machine may be impressive, but since the machine is a separate entity, it is a completely different "person." This new pack of neurons made of fiber optic wire and silicon may act like Ray Kurzweil, and may call itself Ray Kurzweil, but this is no longer the original Ray Kurzweil. Even if we decide to view the machine as "alive" it would be a case of identity theft, not resurrection.

Jewish tradition rejects Francis Crick's hypothesis, and is in agreement with Ray Kurzweil on this point. We are more than a pack of neurons. Aryeh Kaplan's messianic optimism aside, ostensibly it would be a violation of Jewish law to do a complete personality download or to beam someone to a different location if the process would cause the destruction of the original body. According to Jewish law, that would constitute murder. As mentioned above, Kurzweil is not bothered by this technicality.

The controversy hinges on how one determines the criteria for the end of life, an old and ongoing debate in medical ethics. The traditional Jewish view is that death occurs when the soul separates from the body. That was once not so difficult to observe and there was little dispute, but modern medicine and life support techniques have made the issue infinitely more complicated.

Currently the debate exists in cases where the body continues to function while there is no observable consciousness. Ironically, the debate in the future will be when the body ceases to function but consciousness seems to persist. In a case where there is no remnant of the original organic body and the mind has been transferred to a robot, do we declare the person dead and the robot as a new entity? Or is this the same person in a new body?

Experts in Jewish law and Jewish medical ethics have not yet produced a definitive answer to this question. There is reason to suggest that when the original body ceases to function and has no consciousness the body should be treated as a corpse. All of the ritual laws of burial would be observed and the family would be required to observe the laws of mourning as they would for a deceased relative. If the body is considered a corpse, it should stand to reason that the person is dead, regardless of whether there is a consciousness abound that resembles the one that was once in the body.

Philosopher John Searle argues that at some point during the procedure when your neurons are being replaced, you would die. Searle predicts while going through the brain prosthesis, "You find, to your total amazement, that you are indeed losing control of your external behavior. You find, for example, that when doctors test your vision, you hear them say 'We are holding up a red object in front of you; please tell us what you see.' You want to cry out 'I can't see anything. I'm going totally blind.' But you hear your voice saying in a way that is completely out your control, 'I see a red object in front of me.' ... [Y]our conscious experience slowly shrinks to nothing, while your externally observable behavior remains the same."

In a conversation between Alan Dershowitz and Ray Kurzweil discussing the morality of brain transfers, Ray Kurzweil said that eventually we will be able to "scan you[r brain] while you are sleeping and come in the morning and say, 'Good news! We have a new Alan Dershowitz; we don't need the old one anymore!'"

I don't ever want to wake up and be told by Ray Kurzweil, or anyone, that my brain has been scanned so it's now perfectly fine to dispose of me. Unless we can definitively prove that Searle is wrong, I hope that brain scans and downloads remain in the realm of science fiction.

Hi, I'm Ray

Ray Kurzweil has his followers, but he also has his critics. Some are skeptical of the accuracy of his predictions and feel that we are not as close to full brain scans as Ray Kurzweil would have us believe. Physicist Richard Jones in his book, *Against Transhumanism: The Delusion of Technological Transcendence,* asks the question of whether it is possible to map out the wiring diagram of an individual's brain, the map of all the connections between its 100 billion or so neurons. He says that we may be able to do so only for a dead and sectioned brain, but a living brain is an entirely different enterprise for which we have scarcely scratched the surface.

Developmental neuroscientist PZ Myers goes a bit further in his article, "Ray Kurzweil Does Not Understand the Brain." Contrary to the media image of Kurzweil as a genius, Myers insists that Kurzweil is nothing but a new-age guru for technology nerds. He argues that Kurzweil's premises are completely false, and Kurzweil's claims are ridiculous and uninformed. "I'm a developmental neuroscientist; I have a very good idea of the immensity of what we don't understand about how the brain works. No one with any knowledge of the field is claiming that we'll understand how the brain works within ten years. And if we don't understand all but a fraction of the functionality of the brain, that makes reverse engineering extremely difficult...If you're an acolyte of Kurzweil, you've been bamboozled. He's a kook."

But even his fiercest critics must concede that Ray Kurzweil is taken very seriously. Myers writes at the end of his article, "I'll make one more prediction. The media will not end their infatuation with this pseudo-scientific dingbat, Kurzweil, no matter how uninformed and ridiculous his claims get." He goes on to say that critics of Kurzweil are usually answered with accusations of being anti-science religious fanatics, even if the criticism comes from a scientist like Myers. This is what worries me the most.

At some point in the near future we may be confronted with a robot that says to us, "Hi, my name is Ray." The robot may or may not share the appearance of Ray Kurzweil, but it will be programmed with memories from his personal history, it will demonstrate some of his personality traits like his sense of humor or his taste in art or music, and it will claim that it is the real Ray Kurzweil.

The media will no doubt make this a sensational story. Experts like Myers and Jones will write reasoned arguments as to why this is not Ray Kurzweil, but we will be confronted with swarms of Kurzweil followers who will insist it is, and some of those will include highly credentialed and celebrated scientists and technologists.

Those of us who are not experts will be presented with what will appear to be two informed and reasoned sides to a philosophical argument, an argument with immense implications, and we will not know whom to believe.

Wishful Thinking

As tempting as it would be to believe that brain downloads mean the end of death, the fulfillment of Biblical prophecies, and the coming of the Messiah, a few minutes of thought and the application of some common sense quickly dispel that notion. The problem is as you get older and closer to death the idea starts to make more sense. As Richard Jones said, "Why would people think mind uploading will be possible in our lifetimes, given the scientific implausibility of this suggestion? I ascribe this to a combination of over-literal interpretation of some prevalent metaphors about the brain, over-optimistic projections of the speed of technological advance, a lack of clear thinking about the difference between evolved and designed systems, and above all, wishful thinking arising from people's obvious aversion to death and oblivion."

The robot of Ray Kurzweil, no matter how similar to the biological Ray Kurzweil, is nothing more than a copy, no more alive than a photograph, a video, or an anatomic mannequin.

King Saul of the Bible was in dire straits, faced with a battle that seemed insurmountable, and he didn't know where to turn. In his early years he would turn to the prophet Samuel for guidance and encouragement, but Samuel was dead. In desperation Saul hired a necromancer to contact the spirit of Samuel. The woman claimed that she successfully conjured up the ghost of the prophet, which only she could see or hear, and she told King Saul that the spirit was angry with him and predicted his imminent demise.

While some Biblical commentators are open to the possibility that the necromancer had authentic magical powers, it seems obvious that she was just a savvy woman who tricked a desperate King Saul into believing that she had revived his dead mentor, telling Saul exactly what she thought he wanted to hear.

I have no doubt that soon we will have computer programs that can look, act, and even say things that a particular person might say, but Ray Kurzweil can neither bring back his dead father nor bring himself back from the dead by creating a robot replica. He will do no more to abolish death than King Saul's fraudulent necromancer.

Jewish tradition says that every year on Yom Kippur two books are opened up before the heavenly court, the book of life and the book of death. Many people understand this to mean that we are judged as to whether we will live or die in the coming year. But there is the obvious challenge as every year certain wicked people make it through the year, while many righteous people do not.

Rabbi Chaim of Volozyn in the 19th century wrote that this is a misinterpretation of the tradition. What the tradition really means is that the two books are lists of people who will be judged on Yom Kippur. The book of the living contains the names of everyone who is alive in the world today. Each of us is judged based on what we did in the past year. A tally is kept of our good deeds and our bad deeds. Punishment may be meted out in the coming year, it may be deferred to a later year, or the debt will be collected in the world to come. The book of life is not about the reward, it is the status of the defendants.

So what then is the book of death? The book of death is a complete list of all of the people who have ever lived in this world at one point and have since died. Abraham, Moses, and George Washington are all listed in the book of the dead, and they are all judged on Yom Kippur for their actions over the past year. But how can they be judged if they are dead? What actions could they have committed in this past year?

While we are no longer able to affect the world directly after we are dead, our actions during our lifetimes have residual effects. During our lifetime we can inspire others to do good or evil. To a degree, we are responsible if we influence the actions of others, and we are rewarded or punished for those actions, even after we die. A life of goodness that inspires others continues to have an impact long after a person leaves this world. That is the only true way to achieve immortality. There are no short cuts.

3: Rabbi Google

The End of an Era

A rabbi recently posted an article reflecting on the 30th anniversary of the passing of the greatest authority on Jewish law in the latter half of the 20th century, Rabbi Moshe Feinstein. At Rabbi Feinstein's funeral in 1986, one of the eulogizers lamented that we may never see the rise of another rabbi who has the same breadth of knowledge and firm command of the vast collection of Jewish texts that Rabbi Feinstein had.

"Here we are 30 years later, and in fact a rabbi has risen that has access to even more Jewish sources than Rabbi Feinstein. The rabbi's name is Rabbi Google. Today Rabbi Google answers more questions on Jewish law than any rabbi in history."

An electronic brain transfer is one possible path to artificial intelligence. Another is for a super intelligent search engine, most likely Google, to become so smart that it gains self-awareness. Not surprisingly, Google CEO Eric Schmidt predicts that as the internet continues to grow Google will grow in tandem and ultimately develop into a super intelligence that will reflect the collective wisdom of the entire world.

A skeptic would assume that Schmidt is exaggerating as a form of self-serving self-aggrandizement; however, millions if not billions of people, including the rabbi quoted above, speak as if they believe that Google already has a life of its own. The way people feel about Google is subtly reflected in the way people say, "Ask Google," as if Google were not a complex algorithm, but an omniscient oracle.

Professionals, craftsmen, and tradesmen of every kind were once sought after for their knowledge, and were considered by lay people to be unquestionable authorities on their particular areas of expertise. Not anymore. Today, years of study, practice, and experience have been devalued because every person with a laptop or a smartphone and an internet connection can instantly access an entire world of information on any subject just by typing it into the magic search bar.

Google seems to be getting smarter and smarter. As the internet grows, and as searches and traffic increase, Google collects more and more behavioral data that make Google searches more precisely tailored to the user queries. Remember the old days when you actually had to type in the whole sentence? Now you can type just a few letters and Google knows exactly what you want to search. How long before Google gets so smart that it will know what you want to ask before you do?

Behind the idea of the Google super intelligence we find, once again, Ray Kurzweil, currently one of Google's chief engineers, tasked to make computers understand speech. Kurzweil's goal is to enable Google to read, hear, and understand human semantics. "The idea is to create a system that's expert in everything it has read and make that expertise available to the world."

Larry Page, Google's creator and founder, views Google as potentially being sentient. As early as the year 2000, before Google became a household word, Page already said that the ultimate version of Google would be artificial intelligence. In 2003 he said, "The ultimate search engine is something as smart as people – or smarter."

Sergey Brin, the programmer who helped Page create Google, said that the ultimate search engine would look something like Stanley Kubrick's HAL from the classic science fiction thriller, *2001 a Space Odyssey*. "Hopefully," said Brin, "it would never have a bug like HAL did where he killed the human occupants of the spaceship. But that is what we're striving for, and I think we've made it part of the way there." Let's hope that when they get all the way there Brin and Page remember to leave out the "kill humans" feature.

Wisdom of Crowds

According to those who subscribe to the belief in a super intelligent search engine, artificial intelligence does not need to be designed, rather it will evolve and emerge naturally from the collective consciousness of everyone who uses the internet.

This is a version of a theory described by James Suroweiki in his book, *The Wisdom of Crowds: Why the Many Are Smarter Than the Few and How Collective Wisdom Shapes Business, Economies, Societies and Nations*. He opens with an anecdote about a crowd at a county fair that guessed the weight of an ox with unbelievable accuracy when their individual guesses were averaged.

Clay Shirky's book *Here Comes Everybody: The Power of Organizing Without Organizations,* applies the theory to the internet. Since the internet has enabled global collaboration through wikis like Wikipedia, our collective wisdom will produce the best encyclopedia, government, and culture. The theory suggests that the larger the size of the contributing crowd the greater the collective wisdom that will emerge.

The idea of a collective wisdom is not a new one, and dates at least as far back as the Bible. When the Jews were in the desert under the leadership of Moses there was a short-lived rebellion lead by a cousin of Moses named Korach. The rebellion ended badly for Korach, the ground opened up and swallowed him, but initially Korach attracted a significant following. Given that Moses was the leader who freed them after two centuries of Egyptian slavery, it is quite remarkable that Korach was able to incite disloyalty. It is worth exploring what techniques Korach employed to entice people to rebel against a strong leader like Moses.

The Bible sums up Korach's entire campaign against Moses in a single line. "The entire congregation collectively is holy and God is within them, why then do you [Moses] elevate yourself above the people?" While it seems as though Korach was inciting a populist rebellion of the masses against the powerful elites, a careful reading of the text tells a different story. Korach's followers were among those that Moses had appointed as leaders over thousands and ten-thousands. His followers were the powerful elites, yet Korach managed to convince the leadership to turn against itself, advocating against any kind of government or establishment. Korach said, the entire assembly is holy as a collective and God is within that collective. If a prophecy could emerge from Moses, surely a wiki prophecy emerging from the collective would be even better.

Not everyone is convinced that crowds are always so wise. Thomas Jefferson, for instance, wrote that "The mobs of the great cities add just so much to the support of pure government as sores do to the strength of the human body."

As Evgeny Morozov writes, "The fact that no one is in charge does not mean that everyone is free. The authoritarian lion may be dead, but now there are hundreds of hungry hyenas swirling around the body." Instead of wisdom emanating from crowds, what we more often get is what Charles Mackay called "the extraordinary popular delusions and madness of Crowds." Mindless videos about cats attract millions of views on the internet and more attention is paid to the Academy Awards than to the granting of Nobel Prizes. Popularity is not synonymous with wisdom.

The Man Behind the Curtain

What is worse than the madness of crowds is when we are lead to believe that a voice is emanating from the crowd, when in fact it is coming from a small group of people or a single individual.

Those who think that Google is a magical oracle that knows the answer to any question have no understanding of what Google really is. Before the age of the internet it was very difficult to publish an idea. Today everyone with a laptop and an internet connection can publish as much as they want on their own personal blog and share their ideas with the world. While there are obvious advantages to a system where everyone has a voice, the problem is that with so many voices talking at the same time, it gets harder to be heard.

In the old days the major media companies, newspapers, radio, and television stations were the gatekeepers. You could write a letter to the editor, but it was highly unlikely that you would be one of the few that would be published. Today those gatekeepers don't have the power they used to have; they have been replaced by new gatekeepers.

The most powerful of the new gatekeepers is the search engine. Asking Google is not like asking an all-knowing genius. A better analogy to understand Google is to imagine you are sitting in an office across the street from the world's largest library and you hire an assistant who will run across the street and fetch books on a topic that you specify. You don't need to hire an all-knowing genius to fetch the books. You would prefer to hire someone who can run fast so he can quickly fetch you books that were written by experts on the subject of your query. In addition to being a good runner, your assistant would also need to be just smart enough to know how to find the books that best meet your needs. He can only carry a certain amount of books on any given trip, and often there are thousands of possible choices that would be relevant to your query. It would be helpful to understand the criteria that the assistant uses to choose the books that he ultimately decides to bring back to you.

A search engine is your assistant who fetches information from the world's largest collection of information, the internet. Search engines use algorithms to determine which results would respond best to your query. The algorithms were designed by programmers, and they rank web pages based on certain criteria. The exact nature of the algorithms is what makes a search engine unique, so they are kept secret by the search engine companies. Some of the criteria may include the age of the website, the length of the content, or the prevalence of certain keywords. It also includes many other unknown instructions that were decided on by the programmers who designed the algorithms. The websites that meet the most of these criteria end up at the top of the list of results. The sites that meet fewer criteria are buried beneath hundreds of other results.

As Evgeny Morozov characterizes it in his book *The Net Delusion: The Dark Side of Internet Freedom*, "Their version of democracy goes something like this: you enter a voting booth to cast a vote only to discover that the electoral commission is also going to consider your fashion taste, your accent, the weather outside, and many of factors which you cannot be informed about."

If we take the library analogy a step further, now suppose you sent your trusted runner to fetch a cookbook from the library, and while the runner is perusing the shelves and deciding which of the thousands of cookbooks to bring back, he meets a woman who is trying to promote the cookbook she wrote and she pays your assistant five dollars to bring it back to you. Or perhaps he runs into a man who owns the local spice shop, and he pays the runner five dollars to bring you back a stack of cookbooks filled with recipes that require spices that you will likely buy at his store.

You can pay Google to push your website to the top of the list making it more likely that your website will be the answer to someone's query. Alternatively, there is an entire industry called

Search Engine Optimization (S.E.O.) that helps authors and businesses design their websites to meet the algorithm criteria and achieve higher rankings. In our library analogy, it would be like getting a book put on the front and center shelf so that your assistant is more likely to see it and reach for it.

Google can make or break a business with its page ranking. In 2013 a company called Rap Genius was caught by Google using unscrupulous S.E.O. tactics. Google punished the company by moving them from the top of search results to the fifth or sixth page of results, further down the list than anyone is likely to look. Becoming unsearchable was a terrible blow to their business. They weren't behaving so Google affectively kicked them off of the internet. That is a lot of power!

When you enter a query into a search bar the results that you receive are not always the best, and they are not from the crowd. The results are the decisions of the search engine companies, those with the technical knowhow to game the system, and those with the funds to pay them. As Morozov says, the internet is not a democracy, it is an oligarchy.

This is true about social media as well. Contrary to what many people believe, the popularity of social media posts is not always based on the selection of the crowd. If a topic is "trending" on Twitter, it could be because many people are talking about the topic. Alternatively many people could be talking about the topic because it is trending. The algorithms that control what is popular on social media are unknown to us. Social media companies like Facebook and Twitter have been known to manipulate the popularity of posts for political reasons, promoting posts that support a certain political agenda while censoring others that don't conform to their point of view.

Facebook was caught performing psychological experiments on half a million of its users without their knowledge or consent by manipulating what showed up in their news feeds. Half of the experimental group was shown posts with positive keywords while the other half was shown posts with negative keywords. They found that those who were shown positive keywords were more likely to post positive things, and those who were shown negative keywords were more likely to post negatively. The discovery that the crowd is not really in control of what goes viral is almost as disturbing as learning about Facebook's ability to control people's emotions.

Wikipedia is another example of this type of misconception. Wikipedia boasts half a billion unique visitors each month. If that is true, one fourteenth of the world's population is getting its information from one website. Where does that information come from? Some might say that it comes from the crowd, from all of us, yet that is only partially true. In theory anyone can be an editor on Wikipedia. All that a computer user needs to do is open an account. Of the half a billion people who use the site, only 19 million of them have accounts. But of those 19 million accounts, only sixty-nine thousand accounts are active at least once a month (all figures taken from Wikipedia). That means that .0001 percent of Wikipedia users are feeding the content to the rest of the crowd.

Chuck Klosterman said, "The degree to which anyone values the internet is proportional to how valuable the internet makes that person." The executives at the big internet companies would like for us to believe that their supercomputer has a mind of its own. While their computers are very impressive, it is important to recognize that they are still run by algorithms that were programmed by a small handful of people, and not the product of the world's collective consciousness.

The Wisdom of Mrs. Ohn

Korach had a follower named Ohn the son of Pelet. Ohn is mentioned only once at the very beginning of the rebellion against Moses, but then he disappears from the text and we never hear of him again. According to Jewish legend Ohn was saved by his cunning wife. When Ohn returned home after the initial demonstration against Moses, he told his wife all about Korach and his plans for change. His wife was not convinced. "What do you gain from this?" she asked. "Today, Moses is in charge. If Korach wins he will be in charge. Your position will not change." She keenly saw past the illusion that Korach was presenting. The collective consciousness of the crowd wouldn't replace Moses, Korach would.

Moses also saw through Korach's charade. When he learned of the rebellion he prayed, "Almighty God of the spirits of all men; shall one man sin and you be angry at the entire congregation?" Moses saw past the crowds and saw a single man manipulating everyone behind the scenes, and he beseeched God to only punish the man behind the curtain pulling the strings and not the hapless masses that were manipulated by him.

Search engines are a wonderful tool, but we must understand that they are only a tool. If we ascribe undue intelligence to a search engine, a social media platform, or the internet in general, we make ourselves vulnerable to manipulation by those who use these tools to feed us our information.

The use of language can influence the way we think. Rather than say that you read something on Google or on the internet, be specific. From which website did you get your information? The information did not emerge magically from an amorphous crowd. Someone put it there. Behind the search engine and the internet there is a real person who initially crafted the thought and took the time to write it down and share it with the world. To forget that is to humanize the machine and dehumanize the person. The Talmud teaches that one who quotes a saying in the name of the one who said it saves the world. That is true today more than ever before.

4: Turing's Ghost

In Theory

The most direct path towards artificial intelligence is the brute force method, developing a machine that gradually simulates more and more human faculties until the machine's output is indistinguishable from human intelligence.

The Church-Turing Thesis, proposed by Alonzo Church and Alan Turing in the early 20th century, states that "A function on the natural numbers is computable by a human being ignoring resource limitations if and only if it is computable by a Turing machine." As Paul and Patricia Churchland explain the thesis, "A standard digital computer, given only the right program, a large enough memory and sufficient time, can compute any rule-governed input-output function. That is, it can display any systematic pattern of responses to the environment whatsoever."

Said even more simply, there is nothing that a person can do that a sufficiently powerful and intelligent computer cannot also do.

The Church-Turing Thesis raises one of the greatest existential challenges, namely, is there something within man, something mystical, magical, or divine, that makes us human, or are we all just computers following a set of algorithms that could be replicated by a man-made machine?

In his book, *Automate This: How Algorithms Took Over Markets, Our Jobs, and the World*, Christopher Steiner notes that seeds were planted for the Church-Turing thesis as early as the late 17th century, when the great philosopher Gottfried Leibniz developed binary language. In binary code anything can be expressed in the most simplified terms using only zeros or ones. Leibniz theorized that even cognitive thought could be reduced to a series of binary expressions or instructions. The more complicated the thought, the more simple expressions would be necessary to bring them about. The word processor, the smartphone, and the self-driving car are all run by programs consisting of millions of lines of computer code that can be broken down into a long series of binary decisions: on or off, yes or no, one or zero.

Leibniz was a religious man. His idea of binary stemmed from his belief that there are only two absolute truths, God and nothingness. There is either the One True God or there is Zero.

Passing the Test

Are we more than just machines? Francis Crick says no. In his book *The Astonishing Hypothesis*, he wrote that he thinks that we are just a pack of neurons. If a pack of wires and circuits can be programmed to perfectly mimic a man, how is that machine different from a man, and how is a man different from that machine?

The Church-Turing thesis remains a theory until a computer is actually created that is indistinguishable from a person. But what does indistinguishable really mean?

Alan Turing proposed a test that remained the benchmark for researchers of artificial intelligence for decades after his death. The test was introduced by Turing in 1950 in his paper, "Computing Machinery and Intelligence." His paper begins, "I propose to consider the question, 'Can machines think?'"

Turing based his test on a game involving three players. Player A is a man, player B is a woman, and player C, who plays the role of the interrogator, is of either sex. Player C is placed behind a screen and is unable to see or hear either player A or player B, and can communicate with them only by asking questions on written notes. The object of the game is for the interrogator to determine which one of the two players, A or B, is the woman.

Turing's test substituted a computer for the woman, and the interrogator's task was to determine which player was the computer. He theorized that if the interrogator can be fooled as often when the game is played with the computer as when the game is played between a man and a woman it may be argued that the computer is intelligent. Turing also predicted that by the year 2000 a computer smart enough to pass his test would be developed.

A little more than a decade after Turing's paper, Joseph Weizbaum at M.I.T. developed a program called ELIZA, described earlier in chapter one, that was able to fool people into believing that it was a real human therapist. In 1972 Kenneth Colby used a similar but more advanced approach and created PARRY, a program described as ELIZA with attitude. PARRY mimicked the behavior of a paranoid schizophrenic. When groups of psychiatrists were asked to distinguish between transcripts of conversations with PARRY and other conversations with real patients, the results were the same as if they had randomly guessed. They were unable to tell the difference between the patients and a computer program.

However, ELIZA and PARRY were able to pass tests only when the conversations were restricted to certain topics. In any normal human interaction the programs would be exposed for what they are fairly quickly.

In 2014 at an event marking the 60th anniversary of Alan Turing's death, a program called Eugene Goostman was able to fool a sufficient number of human judges in five minute conversations on any topic. This was considered the most advanced Turing test in history, and Eugene Goostman is considered by many to be the first robot to officially pass the Turing Test.

Smart Machines or Dumb Humans

The main criticism of the Turing test is that it doesn't test the computer as much as it tests the human judge. In his book *You are Not a Gadget*, Jaron Lanier points out that we have lowered the bar, making computers more likely to seem human to us. Skeptic Michael Shermer points out that "Human beings consistently choose to consider non-human objects as human whenever they are allowed the chance, a mistake called the anthropomorphic fallacy. They talk to their cars, ascribe desire and intentions to natural forces, and worship the sun as a human-like being with intelligence. If the Turing test is applied to religious objects, inanimate statues, rocks, and places have consistently passed the test throughout history."

The programs that compete in Turing contests are programmed to give responses that mimic certain types of human personas. The ones that tend to do well are not the ones that are programmed to sound intelligent, on the contrary, it's the ones that imitate people of lower intelligence or language abilities. Eugene Goostman speaks like a thirteen-year-old Ukrainian boy who can't speak English very well. Another sophisticated program, McGonz, was programmed to reply to the human judge with hostile strings of profanity, and taunts about the judge's sex life. The tests are less about how smart a computer can be, and more about how willing people are to believe that a person can be so stupid.

The Chinese Room

While we may be a long way from a truly intelligent robot, Turing's question persists. Hypothetically, if one day in the future such a machine were developed, what, if anything, would distinguish the machine from a real person?

Philosopher John Searle insists that it is not possible for a computer running a program to have a mind or a consciousness in the same sense that people do. To substantiate this claim he presented a thought experiment.

Imagine a man locked in a room. The man does not know a single word of Chinese, either written or spoken. The man is given a set of rules in English that enable him to match certain Chinese symbols with other symbols. Outside of the room, fluent Chinese speakers can submit questions, written in Chinese, through a slot in the door. The rules allow him to respond, in written Chinese, to questions, also written in Chinese, in such a way that the posers of the questions are convinced that he can actually understand the Chinese conversation too, even though he cannot.

Similarly, argues Searle, if there is a computer program that allows a computer to carry on an intelligent conversation in a written language, the computer executing the program would not understand the conversation either.

Searle has been debating against proponents of human intelligent robots for decades. He was asked to present his views at Google to an internal Google organization called the Singularity Network that focuses on Artificial Intelligence. Ray Kurzweil attended the lecture.

In his book *The Singularity is Near*, Kurzweil devotes an entire chapter to refuting Searle. Kurzweil points out that Searle's Chinese room argument can be applied to the human brain also. "Although it is clearly not his intent, his line of reasoning implies that the human brain has no understanding. He writes: 'a computer...succeeds in manipulating formal symbols. The symbols themselves are quite meaningless: they have only the meaning we have attached to them. The computer knows nothing of this, it just shuffles the symbols.' Searle acknowledges that biological neurons are machines, so if we simply substitute the phrase 'human brain' for 'computer' we [see that really the computer has or does not have consciousness as much as a human brain does.]"

When Kurzweil posed the question directly to Searle in person, Searle did not offer any formal logical or philosophical answer. He said, "How do I know my dog Tarski is conscious and this thing here, my smartphone, is not conscious? I don't have any doubts about either one…As far as human beings are concerned, there isn't any question. It's not even a theory that I hold. It's a background presupposition. The way I assume that the floor is solid, I simply take it for granted that everybody is conscious."

Kurzweil is not convinced. He responds in his book, "To claim that the computer is not conscious is not a compelling contention. To be consistent with some of Searle's other statements, we have to conclude that we really don't know if it is conscious or not. With regard to relatively simple machines, including today's computers, while we can't state for certain that these entities are not conscious, their behavior, including their inner workings, doesn't give us that impression. But that will not be true for a computer that can really do what is needed in the Chinese Room. Such a machine will at least seem conscious, even if we cannot say definitively whether it is or not. But just declaring that it is obvious that the computer (or the entire system of the computer, person, and room) is not conscious is far from a compelling argument."

John Searle's problem, as Ray Kurzweil points out, is that when all is said and done Searle is a materialist. He is an atheist and does not believe in the human soul. The functions of the computer take place because of a series of syntactical statements, whereas human consciousness is a biological phenomenon. Their inner workings may be different, but if the output is the same, what is the difference? His arguments seem like irrelevant semantics and they do not provide us with a compelling answer to the question of why we should treat an intelligent computer differently than we treat a person.

Who Is I?

Rabbi Joseph Soloveitchik offered a different approach. In a lecture given in Boston about the unity of God as understood by Maimonides, he pointed out that the Biblical assertion "God is one" is not meant as a quantitative statement. It means, as Maimonides explains, that God is completely unified, in all aspects and from every point of view. God's knowledge, God's life, and God's existence are all one."

To explain this, Rabbi Soloveitchik contrasted God's condition with the human condition, which is not unified.

"Everything we know can be described as being external to man. Begin with a random object like a microphone. The microphone is not a part of me. I confront the mike and the mike confronts me. So too, any physical appendage, a hand for instance, can be viewed as external to me. It can be severed physically, or even grammatically. Saying, 'my hand' means that the hand is separate from "my" or from me. I can say it about my hands and my legs, and my heart and my brain. I, subject knower, separate myself from my body which has been identified with me. The body becomes an object of my inquiry."

This exercise of self-knowledge is not limited to physical parts of the body. It can be extended to ephemeral entities such as emotions.

"To quote Descartes, 'I think.' What happens when I make that statement? Immediately in such a case, the knower, the one who formulates the judgment, estranges himself from the 'I' who does the thinking. I feel sad, or happy, or any emotion, there is always the 'I' which is separate. There is no self-knowledge in the full sense of the word. A subject/object confrontation is inevitable."

In contrast to man, God is completely unified. In some mysterious and unknown way God has self-knowledge and it is not severed from His essence. The word "one" in "God is one" is not meant as a quantity, but as a quality.

We think of ourselves in terms of our personalities; however, our personalities can be severed from us. The "I" that is our true essence, our soul, is something deeper; it is something that cannot be scanned and downloaded onto a hard drive. The "I" is more than just the personality, the memory, or the human faculties. Our true essence persists even in absence of the personality, as it does, for instance, in an unfortunate case of severe brain injury. It is something that we do not yet understand, but it is more than a pack of neurons. It is what the skeptical philosopher Gilbert Ryle called the "ghost in the machine."

Nobel Prize winning neurologist John Eccles and philosopher of science Karl Poppers authored a paper called "The Self and the Brain." William Lang Craig explains in a lecture that they understood the material organ known as the brain to be separate from the immaterial unknown substance known to some as the self, and to others as the soul. They explained the relationship between the brain and the self, using an analogy of a pianist and his piano.

"The piano is an instrument that the pianist uses to play music. If the instrument is damaged, or out of tune, or the strings are broken, though pianist has the ability to play good music he won't be able to produce music because the instrument that he uses to make music is damaged or incapacitated. The self and the brain are related in the same way. The brain is the instrument that the self uses to think."

Despite his valiant efforts, John Searle's failure to demonstrate the difference between people and intelligent robots comes from his inability to say outright that he believes that there is something mysterious about the human soul that cannot be detected by our current conceptions of the world. He believes that in theory it is possible to create a machine that can perfectly replicate human consciousness, just not in the way that Kurzweil wants to do it. Kurzweil thinks it can be done with lines of computer code, while Searle believes that the machine would have to imitate our biological functions. They agree in principle, they only disagree on the method.

The Atheist's Dilemma

Professor of philosophy Thomas Nagel sees things differently. In his book *Mind and Cosmos: Why the Materialist Neo Darwinian Conception of Nature is Almost Certainly False,* he writes that "Consciousness is the most conspicuous obstacle to a comprehensive naturalism that relies only on the resources of physical science. The existence of consciousness seems to imply that the physical description of the universe…is only part of the truth." He believes that there is something that makes us human, whatever it is, that is outside of the limits of what we know how to measure. His belief is not based on religion, and he does not attempt to offer an explanation. His point is only that even if we were to learn everything that we could possibly learn about the world with our existing methods, the soul would still remain a mystery. In principle, the soul cannot be understood by our existing methods of inquiry.

"Humans are addicted to the hope for the final reckoning, but intellectual humility requires that we resist the temptation to assume that tools of the kind we now have are in principle sufficient to understand the universe as a whole."

Jaron Lanier says it very well in his book *You Are Not a Gadget*, "If you try to pretend to be certain that there's no mystery in something like consciousness, the mystery that is there can pop up elsewhere." He says that materialist philosophers end up playing a shell game, constantly trying to avoid the mystery by moving it from one abstract concept to another. "Some suppose that consciousness is just a natural outgrowth of time, but by removing mysteriousness from 'consciousness,' you end up mystifying 'time.' The mysterious stuff can be shuffled around, but it is best to just admit when some trace of mystery remains."

Lanier and Nagel are both atheists, but they have the intellectual humility, as Nagel calls it, to recognize that there is something that is still outside of the grasp of what we can currently understand. You don't have to believe in God to believe in the soul.

Atheist writer Camille Paglia expressed a similar idea in an interview.

"I'm speaking here as an atheist. I don't believe there is a God, but I respect *every* religion deeply. All the great world religions contain a complex system of beliefs regarding the nature of the universe and human life that is far more profound than anything that liberalism has produced...There is a huge metaphysical realm out there that involves the eternal principles of life and death."

Most astounding of all, Alan Turing himself wrote explicitly that he believed in the soul. In his seminal paper he wrote, "In attempting to construct such machines we should not be irreverently usurping His power of creating souls, any more than we are in the procreation of children, rather we are, in either case, instruments of His will providing for the souls that He creates."

In conclusion, whether through neural downloads, really smart search engines, or complex thinking machines, one way or another, and at some time in the future, near or distant, we will be confronted with machines that seem to act as smart as we are.

We will be able to device philosophical, semantic, even scientific proofs as to why these robots are not real people, but at the end of the day, if it looks like a person, talks like a person, and acts like a person, people are going to think that it is a person. This is especially true given our tendency to anthropomorphize regular inanimate objects.

Lanier also worries about this. He worries that if enough people pretend that computers are real people and that people are just robots, than perhaps we have the power to make it so.

He equates this with humanity committing suicide for the benefit of a Singularity. Lanier is an atheist, critical of religion and all forms of superstition. He is, however, also aware that by acknowledging that there is something special about consciousness, he contributes to strengthening the position of the dangerous religious fundamentalists. Yet he maintains his position because he believes that engineers like Ray Kurzweil and others that are trying to bring about the Singularity are crazier than religious fundamentalists and pose a greater potential danger to humanity.

5: The Golem of Rehovot

The Legend

"Once upon a time there was a great rabbi in Prague. His name was Rabbi Jehuda Loew ben Bezalel and he is known in Jewish tradition as the Maharal of Prague. A famous scholar and mystic, he is credited by Jewish popular tradition with the creation of a golem—a creature produced by the magical power of man and taking on human shape. Rabbi Loew's robot was made of clay and given a sort of life by being infused with the concentrated power of the rabbi's mind. This great human power is, however, nothing but a reflection of God's own creative power, and therefore, after having gone through all the necessary procedures in building his golem, the rabbi finally put a slip of paper into its mouth with the mystical and ineffable Name of God written on it. So long as this seal remained in his mouth, the golem was alive—if you can call such a state alive. For the golem could work and do the bidding of his master and perform all kinds of chores for him, helping him and the Jews of Prague in many ways. But the poor creature could not speak. He could respond to orders and he could sort them out, but no more than that."

In 1965 the Weitzman Institute installed the State of Israel's first computer. For the dedication ceremony marking this monumental occasion, Dr. Chaim Perekis, the head of applied mathematics at Weitzman and also one of the computer's designers, asked the prodigious scholar of Jewish mysticism, Gershom Scholem, to be the keynote speaker. Scholem began his speech with the story above, the legend of the golem, and per his suggestion Dr. Perekis named the computer The Golem Aleph.

Long ago the legend of the golem made its way into mainstream culture. Gustav Meyrnick, considered by many to be the greatest science fiction writer of the German language, popularized the idea in his widely popular novel *The Golem*. Although never proven, it seems very likely that Mary Shelly's classic *Frankenstein* was based on the golem legends as well.

Gershom Scholem was not the first to make the connection between the creation of the golem and robots. In his lecture he mentioned the Czech playwright Karel Capek and his 1921 play R.U.R. (Rossum's Universal Robots). Capek is credited with coining the word 'robot;' the Czech word 'robota' means 'labor.' Some have suggested that, living in Prague, Capek was inspired by the Jewish tale.

Moshe Idel's book, *Golem: Jewish Magical and Mystical Traditions on the Artificial Anthropoid,* offers a comprehensive survey of the topic.

Sefer Yetzirah

The Hebrew word "golem' originates from the book of Psalms, chapter 139, verse 6, "Your eyes saw my unformed limbs (my golem); they were all recorded in Your book; in due time they were formed, to the very last one of them." The concept of creating artificial men is part of the earliest prehistoric legends of magic; however, the concept of the golem as we know it is not found anywhere in the Bible.

The sages of the Talmud brilliantly employed obscure and cryptic parables, allegories, and riddles to convey certain abstract ideas. In their respective commentaries on the Talmud, authoritative scholars such as Maimonides and Moshe Chaim Luzzatto state that these passages contain important philosophical and ethical principles as well as profound wisdom, and the details are not to be taken literally. One of these passages, found in the Babylonian Talmud, mentions the golem explicitly, and it serves as a perfect example of an ancient parable written almost two thousand years ago that becomes increasingly relevant as we move into the future. "The sage Rabbah created a man and sent his creation to his colleague Rabbi Zera. Rabbi Zera attempted to speak with the man, but he received no answer. There upon Rabbi Zera said to him, 'You must have been made by my colleagues, return to your dust!'"

The surrounding passages mention the study of *Sefer Yetzirah*, *The Book of Creation*, and we can assume that Rabbah consulted it to create his golem.

Sefer Yetzirah is an ancient cryptic manuscript. The date of its authorship is unknown; however, we know that it is at least as old as, if not much older, than the Talmud which was compiled around the 4th century. In Talmudic times only a small elite group of mature scholars were permitted to delve into the study of *Sefer Yetzirah*, and to unlock its profound secrets was considered the pinnacle of scholarly achievement.

The origins and authorship of the mysterious book are also unknown and scholars offer a variety of theories. Some sources identify the author as the Biblical patriarch Abraham. It is written in the book of Genesis that Abraham and his wife Sarah journeyed to the land of Canaan with "the souls they made in the land of Haran." While some commentators understand the verse to be referring to their disciples and followers whom they "made" in a metaphorical sense; there are others who say that the verse is to be taken literally, and that Abraham and Sarah journeyed to the promise land accompanied by a retinue of golems that they created using the secrets of *Sefer Yetzirah*.

In Gershom Scholem's seminal essay, "The Idea of the Golem," he lists numerous legends from Jewish lore about sages that created golems. In the 16th and 17th centuries these stories circulated widely among the Jewish communities of Europe, and Scholem suggests that these stories were influenced less by the short passage in the Talmud and more by the general non-Jewish legends of the Middle Ages.

He cites the story that was told about Solomon ibn Gabriol, the famous poet and philosopher of the eleventh century, that created a woman to wait on him. He was subsequently accused of using magic, which was illegal, but he was able to prove his innocence by deconstructing the robot and showing that she consisted of only wood and hinges.

Most of the golem stories do not involve mechanics, rather the sages would form a man out of clay and then use permutations of the Hebrew alphabet found in *Sefer Yetzirah* to somehow breathe life into the mass of earth and animate their golems.

Stay in the Box

Since Scholem's lecture in Rehovot, the golem has become central to the conversation about Judaism's approach to artificial intelligence. There are some basic similarities between golems and robots. A golem is a man of clay with combinations of letters inserted into its head that bring it to life. A robot is a man of metal with combinations of numbers in its head that bring it to life.

Also, in the Talmudic story about Rabbah's golem, Rabbi Zera applied a test to determine if the golem was real. The test is eerily similar to the Turing test for artificial intelligence. The important similarities are not so much in the construction of the golems, rather they are in the stories about the consequences that emerge from building them.

Man uses technology to create intelligent life only to lose control of his creation and realize too late the dangers involved in playing with powerful forces that are not fully and properly understood. From *Frankenstein*, to *R.U.R.*, to *The Terminator*, this has been a constant theme in popular science fiction for more than a hundred and fifty years. The theme is best demonstrated in the 18th century story, *The Sorcerer's Apprentice,* popularized in the twentieth century in the Disney film, *Fantasia.* In the story the sorcerer's apprentice uses magic to animate brooms to perform mundane household tasks, but the magically animated brooms run amok and cause havoc, until the wise sorcerer returns home and uses his magical know-how to end the spell.

In Jewish folklore there is a golem story with this theme about Rabbi Elijah Baal Shem who lived in the 16th century.

"Rabbi Elijah created his golem by inscribing the word emeth - truth - into the golem's forehead. The golem was very small at first, but would grow in size and strength every day until it was larger than everyone in the house. In order to take away his strength, which ultimately becomes a threat to all those in the house, they must quickly erase the first letter, aleph, from the word emeth on his forehead, so that there remains only the word meth, that is, dead. When this is done the golem collapses and dissolves into the clay or mud that he was…One day, Rabbi Elijah made a golem that became so large that the rabbi could no longer reach his forehead to erase the letter. He thought up a trick, namely that the golem, being his servant, should remove his boots, supposing that when the golem bent over, he would erase the letters. And so it happened, but when the golem became mud again, his whole weight fell on the rabbi, who was sitting on the bench, and crushed him."

The same fears apply to any type of new powerful technology. The first story in the Talmud about *The Book of Creation* is about a group of sages who used the secrets of *The Book of Creation* to create animals which they would slaughter and eat. The future of the Singularity includes the possibilities of radical nanotechnology and the ability to digitize matter and manipulate it to create any object we want. With this kind of technology we will be able to abolish hunger by creating enough food to feed all of humanity.

The downside is the possibility of unintended consequences, like Nick Bostrom's hypothetical case of the "Paperclip Maximizer." Imagine a thoughtless super intelligent machine designed to manufacture paper clips. It keeps manufacturing paper clips, and when it runs out of existing materials it uses nanotechnology to transform the earth and all of its inhabitants into paper clips.

In his book, *Our Final Invention: Artificial Intelligence and the End of the Human Era,* author James Barrat warns us that artificial intelligence is the new existential threat to humanity. He begins with a modern day version of a golem story. Imagine a group of young scientists in Silicon Valley working on a super intelligent computer that is infinitely smarter than the most intelligent human in the world. They create the robot in a sealed computer, not connected to any network, so that the artificial intelligence cannot escape and run amok. The scientists agree on one unbreakable rule. Do not, under any circumstances, connect the supercomputer to any network. The question is, if the robot becomes self-aware and decides on its own that it wants to escape its human gatekeepers, do the humans stand a chance in a battle of wits against something that is more intelligent than anything that humanity has ever encountered?

Barrat doesn't think so. "In a Hollywood film, the odds are heavily in favor of the hard-bitten team of unorthodox A.I. professionals who just might be crazy enough to stand a chance. Everywhere else in the universe the computer would mop the floor with the humans. And the humans have to lose just once to set up catastrophic consequences."

Eliezer Yudkowsky of the Machine Intelligence Research Institute (M.I.R.I.) created something called the A.I. box experiment. Yudkowsky plays the role of a supercomputer that has no physical connection to the outside world, whose objective is to escape the box. His opponent plays the role of the Gatekeeper whose objective is to keep the computer in. Yudkowsky could only communicate to his opponent by text message. He had two hours to escape. Yudkowsky played this game five times for high stakes against famous technology developers. Three out of the five times he escaped. The transcripts to the experiment have remained secret, but Yudkowsky's point is clear. If he could escape even once, a super intelligent robot can almost certainly escape as well.

Like their modern day versions, the tales of the golem were meant as a warning. In the words of Dr. James Hughes, executive director of the Institute for Ethics and Emerging Technologies, "When God jumps out of a box there is nothing that human beings can do to stop or change the course of action."

Jewish tradition incessantly warns that mankind has the potential to bring about its own annihilation. The story of the flood is about how immoral behavior can bring catastrophe and destruction to the world.

God promised that He would not bring another flood, but there is no guarantee that we cannot bring a flood or another kind of massive calamity upon ourselves. Just as we have put a priority on studying the effects of emissions that damage the environment, and as we work against the proliferation of nuclear weapons, we should also prioritize our scrutiny of technology companies and foreign governments that are pursuing artificial intelligence. Thankfully, there are already many influential people who have raised awareness, and I imagine in the coming years this will be something that will be at the forefront of our collective concerns.

Nietzsche's Golem

There are, of course, optimists who are not so easily convinced that artificial intelligence will lead to the apocalypse. Even those who see the potential dangers are also aware of the great benefits that intelligent robots and machines will bring to humanity. To date, machines have provided us with an unprecedented level of comfort. It is impossible to imagine what future comforts technology will bring us. It is at least a possibility that machines will make our lives even better in the future, not destroy us.

There is another danger alluded to in the golem stories that stems not from the potential harm that robots may cause, but from their potential for good.

The generations leading up to the great flood lived lives of unprecedented luxury brought about by their technological inventions. Genesis 4:26 says that it was in the days of Adam's grandson Enosh that man began to attribute divine attributes to inanimate objects. From this verse sprang many Jewish traditions about the origins of idolatry, one of these traditions involve the creation of golems.

Scholem sites a legend in which Enosh inquired from his father Seth about their lineage. Seth informed him that Adam had neither father nor mother, but God had created Adam from

Earth. Enosh went and took a clod of earth and made a figure from it. He said to his father, "But it cannot walk or speak." Seth answered, "God blew the breath of life into Adam's nose." When Enosh proceeded to do this, Satan came and slipped into the figure and gave it the appearance of life, and the generation of Enosh worshiped this figure as an idol.

The lesson of the parable is to be careful not to become too infatuated with the creation of our hands. "Satan" represents the inclination in man that drives him towards evil. In this case, "Satan" leads us to think that our machines are alive. We attribute first human and then ultimately divine characteristics to them until they become objects of worship.

Technologists and programmers that attribute human characteristics to their software, usually do so as a way to inflate the nature of their accomplishment. To create a computer is a great feat for a man, but to create life makes you a god.

Moshe Idel cites another obscure legend linked to the verse about Enosh. "And what did the generation of Enosh do? They went from one end of the world to the other, and each one brought silver, precious stones and pearls in heaps like upon the mountains and hills making idols out of them throughout the world."

This prescient parable immediately brings to mind the modern technology companies like Google, Facebook, and Amazon that have become super powerful through the collection of wealth and information.

The most profoundly relevant story is that of Jeremiah's golem. Jeremiah's son Ben Sira wished to study *Sefer Yetzirah* to create a golem, but a heavenly voice went forth saying, "You cannot make him alone." So he employed the help of his father

Jeremiah and at the end of three years they created a golem. On the golem's head were the words, "Hashem Elohim Emeth." The Lord, God, is truth. The newly created man took a knife and with it he erased the aleph from emeth so that it read, "God the Lord is dead." Jeremiah rent his garments because of the blasphemy and said, "Why have you done this?" The golem replied, "I will tell you a parable. An architect built many houses, cities and squares, but nobody could copy his art and compete with him in knowledge and skill. Two men succeeded to persuade the architect to share his trade secrets with them. After they learned his methods they became architects like him, only they asked for lower fees to build the same buildings. When people noticed this they ceased to honor the architect, and they came to the two men when they required having something built. So God has made you in His image and in His shape and form. But now that you have created a man also, people will say that there is no God in the world." Jeremiah asked the golem, "What should we do?" To which the golem answered, "Destroy me." The two men destroyed the golem that they had created, and Jeremiah said, "Truly one should study these things only in order to know the power of the Creator."

Atheism did not begin with Darwin or with the enlightenment. It is like a fact of nature, as long there are some men who believe in God, there are others who deny His existence. Just as to the religious person the heavens and earth testify to God's existence, to the skeptic the universe seems to prove that there is no God. Mankind's technological prowess can be viewed as a divine gift, and our inventions and achievements as an extension of God's creative hand. Alternatively, our ingenuity can lead to hubris, and, as it says in the book of Proverbs, "Pride goes before the destruction and a haughty spirit before stumbling."

Our lives and the future of humanity are in the hands of those who are most involved in developing the modern golems. Their actions can affect the course of human history for good or for bad. Gershom Scholem wrote, "The source of the danger, however, is not the golem or the forces emanating from him, but the man himself. The danger is not that the golem will become autonomous or will develop overwhelming powers. It lies in the tension which the creative process arouses in the creator himself."

6: Automata

Unspeakable Conversations

Peter Singer is to animals what Ray Kurzweil is to robots. Singer is the ideological father of the animal rights movement, and was instrumental in the movement's revival in the twentieth century. He and his followers advocate for human rights for animals.

Aside from his activism on behalf of animals, Peter Singer is first and foremost a philosopher, known for certain unconventional positions. He has said that it should be legal to kill newborn babies, and people with severe cognitive disabilities at any age. Learning about these positions might lead you to conclude that Peter Singer is evil, and many people would agree. However, many others, including the directors at Princeton University where Singer serves as a professor of Bioethics, consider him a great moral philosopher. Singer is revered in the highest echelons of academia, his books have been translated into dozens of languages and have sold millions of copies, and he is invited to speak to large audiences around the world. Some have gone so far as to call him the greatest philosopher of our time. He is quite possibly one of the most controversial figures alive today.

In 2003, he participated in a public debate with Harriet McBryde Johnson, an attorney and author, who also happens to be disabled from a neuromuscular disease she has had since birth. She is confined to a wheelchair and her body is severely malformed. In her essay for the *New York Times Magazine* titled, "Unspeakable Conversations" McBryde Johnson writes about what it was like to participate in a civilized debate with a man who "insists he doesn't want to kill me. He simply thinks it would have been better, all things considered, to have given my parents the option of killing the baby I once was, and to let other parents kill similar babies as they come along and thereby avoid the suffering that comes with lives like mine and satisfy the reasonable preferences of parents for a different kind of child."

She says that engaging in the debate with him was simultaneously incredibly difficult, and terribly easy. While she was appalled with everything that he said, she found him to be polite and respectful. He was devoid of the usual condescension that most people express towards her, and ironically treated her with respect. She openly admits to being dazzled by his verbal facility.

Singer never wavered from his position that her murder as a baby should have been legal, and yet, by the end of the debate she was shaking and enraged, but not angry at him. She marveled how he had lured her into a civil debate about whether she should exist, and how a packed room of highly educated people could listen politely and not charge the stage and run him out of town.

Speciesism

By what twisted logic can a person so sensitive to the lives of animals be so insensitive to human life? As people continue to attribute human characteristics to robots it will become increasingly important to understand Peter Singer's philosophy. As Peter Singer said, "To end Tyranny we must first understand it."

One of his justifications for infanticide is based on preferences. Singer asserts that a baby born with disabilities is "worse off" than a baby born without disabilities. McBryde, a disabled person herself, argues that Singer is just expressing his own personal preference. She asked him, "What about mixed-race babies, especially when the combination is entirely nonwhite, who I believe are just about as unadoptable as babies with disabilities? Wouldn't a law allowing the killing of these undervalued babies validate race prejudice?" Singer conceded that would be a problem, but held his position because he feels that "Preferences based on race are unreasonable. Preferences based on ability are not." Tell that to the scientist James Watson who believes that black people are less evolved than white people.

Most of us assume that when the interests of a person and an animal conflict, the person should be given "preference." Singer alleges that our preference for a baby over an animal comes from a historical prejudice towards our own species that developed over the last few thousand years. Just as a prejudice against or a preference towards a particular race is called racism, a prejudice against or towards a certain species is called speciesism. In his book, *Animal Liberation: A New Ethics for Our Treatment of Animals*, he gives a concise history of speciesism from ancient times until today.

According to Singer the ancients would use religious, metaphysical, and moral ideas to justify self-serving practices like using animals for food and for clothes. The evolution of our current self-serving attitude towards animals starts with ancient Judaism.

According to the Bible at the time of creation man was given dominion over animals. At first man was not permitted to kill animals for food, but gradually, beginning with the expulsion from Eden, this became acceptable, until it was permitted in a direct proclamation from God after the flood. Singer recognizes that the Bible has many commandments that demand kindliness towards animals, and the early prophets spoke about returning to a utopian future when the wolf and the lamb will lie down together, but the basic position of the Bible is that man stands at the pinnacle of creation above the rest of the animal kingdom.

The Greeks were influenced by the thought of Aristotle. As opposed to the Biblical view that saw mankind standing on a separate higher plane from animals, Aristotle saw all living creatures as belonging to a faded hierarchy, with lower members of the hierarchy created for the sake of the higher beings. Plants were provided by nature for the sake of animals, and animals were created for the sake of men. He also believed that the hierarchy existed within the species of man. He understood there to be different classes of men, and that certain classes with less reasoning abilities were provided as human instruments for the sake of serving men of greater reasoning abilities as slaves.

Aristotle's views laid the groundwork for Western tradition.

The Romans inherited the Greek position but took it to an extreme. They expressed moral concern for those considered the higher classes, but for everything that they considered to be beneath them they demonstrated absolutely no concern. At the infamous Roman games, gratuitous torture and suffering was inflicted upon slaves and animals for no other purpose than entertainment for the "civilized" masses.

Then Christianity came and brought the Jewish idea of the uniqueness of man and the sanctity of human life to the Roman world. Christianity spread the idea that every human life was sacred; however, to emphasize that point it elevated man at the expense of all other creatures, and suppressed the call for sensitivity towards animals mandated in the Jewish Bible.

For example, the Jewish Bible has a number of commandments mandating special treatment for beasts of burden like oxen and donkeys to ensure that they are not subjected to any unnecessary pain or suffering. In the Christian Bible, Paul abrogates men from these laws asking rhetorically, "Does God really care for oxen?" As a result, when Christianity became the dominant religion, to kill or to inflict suffering upon another person was regarded as sinful and hence became taboo, while ill treatment of animals remained morally acceptable, as it was in ancient Rome.

The Circle of Empathy

The development of artificial intelligence will once again force humanity to think seriously about the moral distinctions between humans and members of others species. Philosophers describe a conceptual circle that we draw that encompasses us together with all other people or living things that we consider worthy of our empathy. What falls inside and outside the circle of empathy can tell us a great deal about an individual, a community, or a civilization. In Ancient Rome free men were inside the circle, while slaves, criminals, prisoners, and foreign captives were out. Along came Christianity and suddenly all people were invited into the circle, but animals were still out.

Over the centuries the world has gradually drifted back to the Jewish view that animals should reside on the periphery of the circle. They are not completely in, but Judaism showed moral concern for animals so long as their interests do not conflict with the interests of man.

Then Charles Darwin came with his theory of evolution, particularly the idea that all creatures share a common ancestor. Peter Singer understands the implications of Darwin's theories to mean "Human beings now knew that they were not the special creation of God, made in the divine image and set apart from the animals...It can no longer be maintained by anyone but a religious fanatic that man is the darling of the whole universe, or that other animals were created to provide us with food, or that we have divine authority over the animals and divine permission to kill them."

Singer argues that Darwin's theories show that it is self-evident that the circle of human concern should be expanded to encompass animals fully. No longer is it morally acceptable to keep animals at the outer rim of our circle where their welfare is completely disregarded just because they happen to taste good.

What seems self-evident to Singer is not so obvious to others. Accepting Darwin's theory does not automatically lead one to conclude that there is no God and that we must all be vegetarians. There is no contradiction in simultaneously believing in evolution on the one hand and a Creator who guided evolution and imbued mankind, not animals, with a divine soul. Parenthetically, Charles Darwin was not a vegetarian.

In order for Darwin's theory to reach Singer's conclusions, you must accept another premise along the way, the astonishing hypothesis of Francis Crick. If there is no divine soul and humans are just a pack of neurons, then it follows that we are no different from any other pack of neurons.

The problem is if you keep traveling down that road you pass right by Peter Singer and arrive at the conclusion of atheist Christopher Hitchens who wrote in his book, *God is Not Great*, "When it comes to the whirling, howling wilderness of outer space, with its red giants and white dwarfs and black holes, its titanic explosions and extinctions, we can only dimly and shiveringly conclude that the 'design' hasn't been imposed quite yet, and wonder if this is how dinosaurs felt when the meteors came smashing through the earth's atmosphere and put an end to the painless bellowing rivalry across primeval swamps…Meanwhile, the sun is getting ready to explode and devour its dependent planets like some jealous chief or tribal deity. Some design!" If we are all just a pack of neurons randomly floating around in space and about to be incinerated in the fallout of a supernova, one wonders why we should have empathy for anything at all.

Empathy Inflation

Singer wrote a book called *The Expanding Circle*. The problem is as the circle expands we get what Jaron Lanier calls empathy inflation. When all life is considered to have equal value, rather than elevate the level of empathy for all, we tend to spread our empathy thin and distribute an equally depressed level of empathy across the board.

Philosopher Rene Descartes saw animals as what he called automata, meaning they act as if they have a soul, but in fact they are nothing more than a watch made of biological materials. Screams of pain from an animal are just the output of a machine, nothing for a person to be concerned about.

We have seen what happens when humans are considered automata. The Nazis were able to commit acts of unspeakable cruelty towards defenseless men, women and children, because they sufficiently dehumanized the Jewish People to the point that they saw them as no more than automata. The screams of the victims sounded like the screams of real people, but the Nazis regarded them as sounds from a machine that had no real feelings and that merited no human concern.

Peter Singer is not the first to flirt with the idea of expanding the circle to include animals. In his article "Vegetarianism and Judaism," Rabbi J. David Bleich cited the fifteenth century Jewish philosopher, Joseph Albo, who wrote "The renunciation of the consumption of meat for reasons of concern for animal welfare is not only morally erroneous but even repugnant." Albo suggested that the people before the great flood adopted this philosophy. Rather than lead to the cessation of violence towards animals, it lead to the acceptability of violence against fellow men. Subsequent to the flood, meat was permitted to Noah in order to impress upon mankind the superiority of man over animals.

One Jewish thinker who is often cited as being favorable towards vegetarianism is Rabbi Abraham Isaac Kook. Rabbi Kook mentions in his writings that vegetarianism represents an ideal that man may one day achieve in the days of the messiah. However, Rabbi Bleich points out that Rabbi Kook spoke out against trying to impose vegetarianism as an ideal on contemporary society. As if predicting the rise of Peter Singer, Rabbi Kook argued that if man were to confer the same rights upon animals that are afforded to people it would not elevate the status of people, it would denigrate the status of man, giving man license to think that he is bound to the same morality of brute animals.

A Still Small Voice

Steven Weiss, head of the Nonhuman Rights Project (NhRP), applies the philosophy of Peter Singer to the real world. Weiss and his fellow advocates are working toward getting animals to be recognized as having legal rights similar to humans. Their stated mission is "to change the common law status of at least some nonhuman animals from mere 'things,' which lack the capacity to possess any legal right, to 'persons,' who possess such fundamental rights as bodily integrity and bodily liberty, and those other legal rights to which evolving standards of morality, scientific discovery, and human experience entitle them." They have filed a number of lawsuits on behalf of animals in captivity, hoping that a court will one day recognize the petition of an animal as they would a human.

In the not too distant future, we may see the emergence of a similar group that will be advocating on behalf of robots. The suits filed by the NhRP on behalf of animals are based on testimonies and affidavits filed by scientists providing evidence demonstrating that the animals are self-aware and autonomous. It is not hard to imagine similar "scientific evidence" provided in affidavits and testimony by experts like Ray Kurzweil and others who want to see robots treated as people.

On the one hand, it would seem that including animals into our circle of moral concern would be more likely than including robots. Animals have been around as long as humans, we may share common ancestry, and we have similar biological makeups. On the other hand, an intelligent robot will demonstrate a form of intelligence far more similar, if not superior, to our own. Even the most intelligent primate trained to communicate in sign language would still require a human advocate to assist him or her in presenting a petition. The intelligent robot, by contrast, will be able to present its petition better than the best attorney.

Jaron Lanier acknowledges that some people seem to hear these small voices that emanate from animals that demand the same empathy that we would afford to humans, but he is not ashamed to admit that he does not hear those voices himself. Other people seem to be hearing those same small voices from algorithms, search engines, and robots. Lanier doesn't hear the voices from animals that would morally compel him to abstain from meat, nor does he hear the voices from computers suggesting that they are alive, conscious, or human. The situation can become frightening when only some people hear certain voices while others not at all, as it could lead to a confrontation where a small and powerful group seeks to impose its own metaphysical ideas onto others. A scene from George Orwell's *1984* comes to mind, in which the protagonist

Winston Smith is mercilessly tortured by the regime operative until Winston declares that he truly believes that two plus two is five.

On the other hand, in an argument similar to Pascal's wager, what if the animal and robot activists are right? For most of human history slavery was deemed moral because slaves were considered subhuman. Plato, Aristotle, even Maimonides believed that within the species of man there were hierarchies which today we utterly reject. As late as 1906 the Monkey House at the Bronx Zoo in New York shamefully featured an exhibit with a black man by the name of Ota Benga.

As Steven Weiss points out, "Not long ago, people generally agreed that human slaves could not be legal persons, but were simply the property of their owners. We are asserting, based on clear scientific evidence, that it's time to take the next step and recognize that these nonhuman animals cannot continue to be exploited as the property of their human 'owners.'"

Currently we are comfortable denying computers personhood, but maybe someday we will look back on our present conceptions with embarrassment. Perhaps the next step in the moral evolution of humanity would be to recognize that robots are people too.

On the cusp of the Civil War, Rabbi M.J. Raphall at Congregation B'nei Jeshurun in New York gave a sermon in defense of slavery. Not because he believed slavery to be moral. He did not. "My friends, I find, and I am sorry to find, that I am delivering a pro-slavery discourse. I am no friend to slavery in the abstract, and still less friendly to the practical working of slavery...[but] with a due sense of my responsibility, I must state to you the truth and nothing but the truth, however unpalatable or unpopular that truth may be."

Prior to the industrial revolution every civilization relied on slaves. Before the invention of machines that worked for us, slaves were the only practical method to harvest crops, build a city, and perform a host of other essential tasks that made civilization possible. Given the reality of the world in which they lived, philosophers of those days would work backwards to justify the institution.

The Bible makes no apology for slavery because in the time it was written there was nothing to apologize for. "Abraham, Isaac, Jacob, Job—the men with whom the Almighty conversed, with whose names He emphatically connects His own most holy name, and to whom He vouchsafed to give the character of perfect, upright, fearing G-d and eschewing evil" were all slave owners.

Rabbi Raphall spoke to an audience of Northerners who only recently had experienced the beginning of the industrial revolution that created a world in which slaves were no longer necessary to enjoy the luxuries of modern life. Their fathers and grandfathers did not share their moral outrage towards slavery; they may have even been slave-owners themselves. "You [may] answer me, 'Oh, in their time slaveholding was lawful, but now it has become a sin,' I in my turn ask you, 'When and by what authority you draw the line?' Tell us the precise time when slaveholding ceased to be permitted, and became sinful?"

It was technology, not philosophy that brought the Northerners to the conclusion that slavery was morally repugnant. Rabbi Raphall's argument was that just as the Northern economy was no longer reliant on slavery and therefore Northern residents no longer sought to justify the institution, sooner or later technology would make human slavery obsolete in the South, and at such time slavery would be rejected there as well. He criticized the Northerners for condescending to the Southeners with an unearned sense of self-righteousness, "solely because they exercise a right which your own fathers and progenitors, during many generations, held and exercised without reproach or compunction."

He was against slavery, but he, like those who opposed the Iraq War in the twenty-first century, was more opposed to a war that would weaken our country, wreck our economy, and cause the death of millions of people, including many of the people they were fighting to free. He agreed with the cause, but disagreed with the method in bringing it about. The goal, as he saw it, was to get the Southeners to hear the same voices of humanity emanating from the slaves that the Northerners heard, but to do so without resorting to a bloody civil war.

The Bible allowed for slavery, but in the book of Exodus and subsequent legal codes, strict sanctions are placed on slave owners. "The law, in permitting him to be sold, contemplated his restoration to his full rights, it took care that during his servitude his mind should not be crushed to the abject and cringing condition of a slave...Thus he is fenced round with protection against any abuse of power on the part of his employer; and tradition so strictly interpreted the letter of the law in his favor, that it was a common saying of Biblical times and homes, which Maimonides has preserved to us, that 'He who buys a Hebrew bondman gets himself a master'...His female slave was not to be the tool or castaway toy of his sensuality...His male slave was protected against excessive punishment…thus two of the worst passions of human nature, lust and cruelty, were kept under due restraint…This, indeed, is the great distinction which the Bible view of slavery derives from its divine source. The slave is a *person* in whom the dignity of human nature is to be respected; *he has rights.* Whereas, the heathen view of slavery which prevailed at Rome, and which, I am sorry to say, is adopted in the South, reduces the slave to a *thing*, and a thing can have no rights."

Rabbi Raphall's alternative to war was, "If our Southern fellow-citizens would adopt the Bible view of slavery, and discard the heathen slave code, which permits a few bad men to indulge in an abuse of power," slavery would become economically unviable, and perhaps necessity would prompt technological innovation that would abolish slavery altogether. In that scenario Southern slavery would die out on its own accord without a single shot fired.

Rabbi Raphall's solution is fine for the oppressors, but is lacking from the perspective of the oppressed. It says to the slaves of the south, "Have patience. Eventually you will be treated as people. Trust us." I don't know if I would be okay with that if I were a slave.

While Peter Singer has definitely worked to move the needle in favor of animal rights, we are a very long way from granting animals full rights. Despite all of the progress that has been made in the last 40 years, the meat industry is doing better than ever. If artificial meat is ever as tasty and affordable as real meat it may change the way we view animals. We may all start hearing those small voices and look back in shame at the times when people thought killing animals for food was morally acceptable. Peter Singer doesn't want to wait for that, and I imagine, neither do cows.

In cases where only a small group hears a particular voice calling for empathy, we have no choice but to adopt the position of Rabbi Raphall. We must apply the Biblical principles of kindness, even if we don't offer full rights. As the voices become clearer and the number of people who hear the voices increases, we can begin to reconsider.

The Talmud tells a story about the great sage Rabbi Judah who was once walking in the market place when a young calf, about to be slaughtered, escaped and tried to hide under Rabbi Judah's robe. Instead of providing the animal with sanctuary, Rabbi Judah pushed the animal away and said, "Go, for this purpose you were created." Rabbi Judah was punished for his callousness. Not because Judaism demands abstention from meat, but because he lacked empathy for something that acts like a living creature. In the most disturbing scene of Steven Spielberg's movie *A.I.,* a group of anti-robot activists demonstrates their disdain for artificial humans by subjecting them to torture and destruction, but when the robot that appears to be a young boy released cries of terror, the group, despite themselves, was moved to mercy.

The philosopher Immanuel Kant believed animals were automata, but he maintained that we have a responsibility to treat them with sensitivity, not for their sake, but because our treatment of them can affect the way we treat other people.

The same idea is invoked in Jewish tradition. When Moses was told to smite the Nile with his staff in order to turn the water to blood, he assigned the task to his assistant. The commentator Rashi explains that since the river had saved him as a baby it was appropriate for Moses to demonstrate an extra level of sensitivity towards the Nile. Not because Moses shared the idolatrous anthropomorphic notions of the Egyptians, rather because he habituated himself with the attribute of gratitude.

We must not be pressured by others into believing that machines are alive. However, if there does emerge a type of machine that can perfectly imitate human actions, and if it appears that the machine is experiencing pain, we cannot ignore what appears to be suffering, even if we know that the suffering is just the output of a machine. To do so would have a negative effect on our personalities, and would cause us to become callous towards human suffering.

Whether we like it or not, I am certain that in the future we will be forced to expand our circle of empathy and show sensitivity towards robots. When machines reach a certain level of intelligence we will not be able to deny them their humanity without seriously damaging our own. But as we let mechanical newcomers enter our circle of empathy, we must vigilantly ensure that we don't displace our fellow man.

7: Love Your Robot as Yourself

A.I. Do

In 2015, in a five-to-four decision, The United State Supreme Court held that the fundamental right to marriage is guaranteed to same-sex couples by the Fourteenth Amendment. According to the majority opinion, the *Obergefell v. Hodges* decision was based on certain "principles and traditions" such as individual autonomy and the right to personal choice. The landmark decision may have set the precedent needed for the eventual legalization of robot marriage.

The court listed a number of reasons why same-sex couples should be able to marry, and all of them could easily be applied to an intelligent robot. The first principle, "The right to personal choice regarding marriage is inherent in the concept of individual autonomy," on its own would open up the door to any sort of marriage that a person chooses.

The court added that the fundamental right to marriage is important in the "safeguarding of children and families." That could be applied more so to robots than to people, as Isaac Asimov argued in his short story in *I Robot* about a robotic nursemaid. "A robot is infinitely more to be trusted than a human nursemaid. Robbie was constructed for only one purpose really – to be a companion of a little child. His entire 'mentality' has been created for the purpose. He just can't help being faithful and loving and kind. He's a machine – made so. That's more than you can say for humans."

The real question of robot marriage is whether it is between two "persons." In the words of the decision, "Marriage responds to the universal fear that a lonely person might call out only to find no one there. It offers the hope of companionship and understanding and assurance that while both still live there will be someone to care for the other."

Robots are already smart enough to fool people into thinking that they are human. It does not take a stretch of the imagination to conceive of a person "falling in love" with their robot, and it is not for the courts to decide what it means to be "in love."

The court ruled that the right to marry is fundamental because "It supports a two-person union unlike any other in its importance to the committed individuals." Regarding robot marriage, the only question left for the court to decide is whether or not a robot can be considered a "person."

In their paper "Robotic Marriage and the Law," Moshe Goldfeder and Yosef Razin demonstrate that a robot can indeed be considered a "person" in the eyes of the law.

"The establishment of personhood is an assessment made by a legislature or a judicial body to grant an entity rights and obligations, regardless of how the entity looks and whether or not it could pass for human. The truth is that the notion of personhood has expanded significantly, albeit slowly, over the last few thousand years. Throughout history, women, children, and slaves have all at times been considered property rather than persons. The category of persons recognized in the courts has expanded to include entities and characters including natural persons aside from men...as well as unnatural or juridical persons, such as corporations, labor unions, nursing homes, municipalities and government units."

Black's Law Dictionary defines an artificial person as "an entity created by law and given certain legal rights and duties of a human being; a being, real or imaginary, who for the purpose of legal reasoning is treated more or less as a human being." Accordingly, the court can choose to consider an artificial intelligence as an artificial person.

The limits to the ramifications of artificial personhood have been pushed in test cases for years. For more than ten years activist Jonathan Frieman of San Rafael, California had been trying to get pulled over for driving alone in the carpool lane. When a police officer finally pulled him over, Frieman waved his corporation papers at the officer. Frieman argued in court that the restrictive highway signs said that two "persons" must be in the car to use the lane, and according to California state law, a corporation is a "person."

Like same-sex marriage, the courts will accept robot marriage when society begins to perceive robots as people, not based on legal semantics. A robot wedding between two robots has already taken place in Japan, and many predict that it won't be long before it makes its way to the United States. Writer Gary Merchant wrote, "While few people would understand or support robot-human intimacy today, as robots get more sophisticated and humanlike, more and more people will find love, happiness, and intimacy in the arms of a machine. Robot sex and love is coming, and robot-human marriage will likely not be far behind."

Who's Your Mama?

The question of robot personhood has legal, moral, and religious applications that will most certainly become a focus of our attention in the coming years. Azriel Rosenfeld, a rabbi and professor of computer science, started posing these questions in the 1960s.

"A robot which can pass Turing's Test will, ipso facto, be in an excellent position to claim that it is entitled to all the rights and privileges of a human being. 'Hath not a robot...dimensions, senses, affections, passions?' Such a robot will almost certainly demand civil rights, union hours, the right to vote. Moreover, such a robot will of course make the claim that it has free will – in fact, that it has an immortal soul. There are no scientific grounds for rejecting these claims; the soul is not directly detectable by physical means. Can they be rejected on religious grounds? If a robot demands religious rights, if it asks to be accepted as a proselyte, is it conceivable that its request could be honored?"

In a secular court based on current legal precedent it would be harder to argue against robot marriage than to argue for it. Based on our experience with the debate over same-sex marriage one would think it would be a much harder sell in a religious court, but that is not necessarily so. Robot marriage is not based on a prohibition; it is only based on the definition of personhood. There are some authoritative traditional sources that have argued liberal definitions for personhood, and based on those arguments a good case could be made to include robots.

What makes something a person according to Jewish law? The sources are clear that a human form is not a requirement for personhood. In the 16th century Rabbi Eleazar Fleckeles of Prague was asked what should be done about a child born to a human woman that did not appear to have a human form. In his ruling Rabbi Fleckeles insisted that the child was human in every regard, "Let no man, by any means, stretch out his hand to hurt the child or to cause its death indirectly; to do so comes under the heading of murder."

Although this may have been a controversial matter in earlier centuries, it is fair to say that contemporary moral sensibilities dictate that any living child born to a human mother is a human, regardless of its form. What about something that does not emerge from a human mother?

The sages of the Talmud debated the status of animals that appeared to have certain human characteristics or abilities. There was a creature known as the *Adnei Hasadeh,* which one 19th century commentator suggested could have been the orangutan, and another known as the *Dulfan,* which some suggest may be a dolphin. These creatures expressed either what appeared to be human intelligence, or the ability to procreate with humans. Despite the unusual nature of these phenomena, the sages ruled that these animals are not to be considered human.

Some suggest that the reason these animals are not considered human is because they were not born from a human mother, and a number of Jewish legal authorities take this definition of "person" to be authoritative fact. This would be consistent with many places throughout the Bible and Talmud where humans are referred to with a term that means, "those born of a woman."

Moshe Goldfeder, in his paper "Not All Dogs Go to Heaven: Judaism's Lessons in Beastly Morality," rejects this position and points out that this definition leads us to a startling conclusion, namely, since Adam and Eve were not "born of a woman" they are not human, and since we are descendants of nonhumans, ergo we are not human either.

The contradiction can be solved by suggesting that those authorities would redefine "born of a woman" to mean having human DNA. "The biblical usage of that phraseology may have been a simple way of referring to the usual method of possessing precise human biological specifications, but not necessarily the only one." This definition would then include children formed in vitro, and possibly human clones, but would not include a robot.

In his article "Cloning People and Jewish Law," Michael Broyde, Rabbi and Professor of Law, provides an alternative definition from the Jerusalem Talmud that supports a definition of humanness that may be applied even in cases where the term "born of a woman" cannot.

"Rabbi Yasa states in the name of Rabbi Yochanan: 'If [a creature] has a human body but its face is of an animal, it is not human; if [a creature] has an animal body, but its face is human, it is human...Yet suppose it is entirely human, but its face is animal like, and it is learning Torah? Can one say to it 'come and be slaughtered'? Or consider if it is entirely animal like, but its face human, and it is plowing the field [acting like an animal] do we come and say to it, 'come and perform levirate marriage and divorce?'""

Rabbi Broyde concludes, "When dealing with a 'creature' that does not conform to the simple definition of humanness – born of a human mother – one examines context to determine if it is human. Does it study Torah (differential equations would do fine for this purpose, too) or is it at the pulling end of a plow?"

According to this definition, it would seem that a robot with human intelligence should be legally treated as a person, at least for civil matters. That could potentially imply that the robot should not be killed or caused to suffer, and perhaps robots would have additional legal rights, privileges, and responsibilities such as the ability to acquire property and liability for any damages it causes.

The question gets more interesting when we think about ecclesiastic matters. Can a robot convert to Judaism? If it is powered by electricity would it have to shut itself down for the Jewish Sabbath? Would it count as part of a quorum of ten required for Jewish prayer? If robot marriage is deemed legal, how do we determine the robot's gender?

These latter questions are the type that Jewish law is quite capable of dealing with, and much of Jewish legal discussion is about applying ancient principles to modern technology. The scholarly community welcomes and indeed revels in these types of discussions, and lively debates on some of these matters already exist. Moshe Idel's book on the golem has an entire chapter entitled "The Golem in Jewish Law" that is a comprehensive survey of these and other similar questions that were debated by Jewish legal scholars hundreds of years ago.

The subject becomes less comfortable when dealing with the allocation of resources and questions of life and death. If a human and a robot are in danger and only one can be saved, should the human take precedence over the robot or are they considered equal? Would you be obligated to risk your own life to save a robot? Should charitable funds be given for the welfare of robots? What if those funds would be given at the expense of the welfare of people?

In the case of the corporate papers in the California carpool lane mentioned above, the court ruled that even though technically speaking the law may sometimes consider a corporation to be a person, in the case of the carpool lane the intent of the law clearly precludes such treatment. Even if it could be proven that robots are technically "people" according to the letter law, syllogisms alone would make them no more human than Frieman's corporate documents. In order to fully consider robots as humans in every instance, we would need more to go on.

8: Why is This Byte Different From All Other Bytes?

Domo Arigato, Rabbi Luzzatto

How are people different than machines? That's easy. People have souls, machines do not. Now all we need to do is define exactly what we mean when we talk about the "soul."

According to Jewish tradition the soul is that divine spark within every person that makes us unique from the rest of creation. The sages of the Talmud wrote that the human soul shares five things in common with God. "Just as God fills the entire world, the soul fills the entire body. Just as God sees but is not seen, the soul sees but is not seen. Just as God sustains the entire world, the soul sustains the entire body. Just as God is pure, the soul is pure. Just as God resides in a chamber within a chamber, the soul resides in a chamber in a chamber."

The main commonality between the soul and God is that both cannot be measured by our current instruments, or described by our current methods of scientific inquiry. Accordingly, the soul is not our personality, which can be measured and observed as part of our physical brain. Damage to the brain or loss of memory can alter a person's personality, but even someone in an irreversible coma is still considered to have a soul.

The eighteenth century philosopher Rabbi Moshe Chaim Luzzatto outlines a traditional Jewish approach to the soul in *The Way of God*, his comprehensive survey of Jewish thought. Like Descartes who believed that the world consisted of two kinds of substance, matter (*res extensa)* and mind (*res cogitans)*, Rabbi Luzzatto believed the world is made up of the spiritual and the physical. "The spiritual consists of all entities which are not physical and which cannot be detected by physical means."

The same dichotomy could be applied to the soul. "Man's soul is comprised of two different components that represent two different types of souls. One type of soul that man has is the same as that which exists in all living creatures. It is this animal soul that is responsible for man's natural feelings and intelligence…This type of soul, often referred to as '*nefesh*,' is transmitted when the seed takes root at the time of conception, and then continually spreads, constructing a body appropriate for each particular species. As the creature matures, it continues to grow, and it is responsible for the existence of its senses, as well as the intelligence appropriate for the particular species…In man's animal soul, certain attributes and faculties can also be distinguished. These include his imagination, memory, intelligence and will. All of these faculties contained in this animal soul, each one having its own particular domain and unique function."

According to the Bible, the *nefesh* resides in the blood of an animal. It is the physical part of the soul that is not unique to man, and can be said to be the physical genetic code in each of us. In his modern translation of *The Way of God*, Rabbi Aryeh Kaplan actually uses the term "genetic material."

It seems to me that it would not be inconsistent with the words of Rabbi Luzzatto to say that a robot can have a *nefesh*. Instead of genetic code, a robot's *nefesh* would be the programming code that would give the robot the characteristics perceived in its output. The *nefesh* is not what makes man different from animals, and I don't see how the word "*nefesh*" could not be used to describe that force which causes a robot, like an animal, to "follow its natural laws according to the availability of the instruments at its disposal," as Rabbi Luzzatto says.

In a certain sense, Rabbi Luzzatto is like Descartes and others who believed that animals were a form of automata. Animals have a type of physical "soul" that gives them life and animation, but they are lacking a spiritual component that makes them human. I don't see anything heretical about applying the same idea to robots.

Rabbi Luzzatto goes on to describe the second type of soul. "Besides the [*nefesh*], however, there exists in man a spiritual entity that is very different and much higher than this animal soul." This is the spiritual soul, referred to as the *"neshamah."* The word *neshamah* probably derives its root form the Hebrew word for breath, as in the Biblical story of creation where God "blew a soul into man's nose."

"The *neshamah* directs man's animal soul. It guides this lower soul, forming mental images in it according to its readiness. It also initiates thoughts and desires according to the direction towards which it inclines...It has experiences relating to its nature. Even though it is bound to the body, it still has some access to the spiritual which is not precluded by its association with the body. The spiritual association of the *neshamah,* however, only has the barest minimal effect on the human mind and its thoughts...What this means is that this person's divine soul has access to certain information, but a complete picture is not transmitted to the thoughts and intellect. The individual therefore experiences no more than the slightest impression."

The *neshamah* is the part of us that connects us to God. It directs us, but it cannot be measured by physical means. The impact that the *neshamah* has on our mind and thoughts, no matter how minimal, is that which separates us from animals and robots.

Speak to Me

The most obvious outward differentiation between human intelligence and animal intelligence is the human ability to speak. According to the ancient and authoritative Biblical translation of Onkelos, when God breathed a living soul into man, it means that man was given the capacity to speak.

This means more than just the ability to talk. A parrot can enunciate words, but that does not mean that it has a *neshamah*. In 1978 Texas instruments developed an educational toy for children called the Speak and Spell. The Speak and Spell contained a processing chip along with a speech synthesizer, a computer program with the ability to produce artificial human speech. The first speech synthesizers were developed as early as the 18th century, and nobody argues that they are human.

In a Talmudic passage quoted earlier, Rabbah created a golem and sent it to his colleague Rabbi Zera. Rabbi Zera performed his version of the Turing test on the golem, and when he determined that the golem could not speak Rabbi Zera destroyed it. Many commentators suggest that Rabbi Zera was not testing for any kind of speech, rather he was testing for the capacity for intelligent speech.

In his essay, "Consciousness in Human-Level A.I.," Murray Shanahan wrote, "Surely nothing would count as having human level intelligence unless it had language, and the chief use of human language is to talk about the world. In this sense, intelligence is bound up with what philosophers call intentionality. Moreover, language is a social phenomenon, and a primary use of language within a group of people is to talk about the things they can all perceive (such as this tool or that piece of wood), or have perceived (yesterday's piece of wood) or might perceive (tomorrow's piece of wood, maybe)."

Similarly, the eminent Biblical commentator Rashi writes in his commentary to Genesis 2:7 that the difference between man and animal is that man has not only speech, but speech and intelligence.

We find that in order to isolate the uniqueness of the irreplicable human soul we must isolate the uniqueness of irreplicable human intelligence, a task that may be just as difficult.

What's Daat?

The Bible uses three main words for intelligence: *Chokhmah*, *Binah*, and *Daat*.

The words appear in the thirty-first chapter of the book of Exodus by the construction of the Tabernacle. *Chokhmah*, sometimes translated as wisdom, is defined by the commentator Rashi as "what a man hears from others and learns." *Binah*, translated as understanding, is defined as "one who understands things on his own out of things that he has learned." Wisdom is a collection of pure thought, whereas understanding represents the ability to utilize the thoughts and parse them into differentiated ideas. As Aryeh Kaplan explained it in his commentary to *Sefer Yetzirah*, "An example would be water flowing through a system of pipes. The water itself is an undifferentiated fluid, having no essential (macrocosmic) structure. Structure is only imposed on it when it flows through the system of pipes. In the analogy, wisdom is the water while understanding represents the pipes that channel it."

There are already computers that have wisdom and understanding far superior to any human, without being human. IBM's Watson, for example, is a question answering computer system capable of answering questions posed in natural language. In 2011, Watson competed on the quiz show *Jeopardy!* and defeated the all-time best human players.

Watson operates in two stages. First, Watson has access to 200 million pages of structured and unstructured content. That is a stack of papers 68,000 feet high. The sources of information for Watson include encyclopedias, dictionaries, thesauri, articles, literary works, and the full text of Wikipedia. The data storage is Wisdom.

Next, Watson parses questions into different keywords and sentence fragments in order to find statistically related phrases by simultaneously running hundreds of proven language analysis algorithms. After running these different searches simultaneously, if many algorithms find a possible answer independently, it gives the potential answer a higher percentage of success. The ability to delve into its store of wisdom and provide an answer to a specific question demonstrates a certain level of understanding.

Philosophers including John Searle point out that Watson does not actually have human intelligence. Watson was designed only to manipulate symbols, but these symbols have no "meaning" to Watson. "Watson did not understand the questions, nor its answers, nor that some of its answers were right and some wrong, nor that it was playing a game, nor that it won – because it doesn't understand anything."

Searle points out that the computer only simulates human understanding, but it is completely different from the brain. The brain has something that he calls "consciousness." That is what he says separates human understanding from Watson's simulation of understanding.

A computer may display output that seems indistinguishable from human behavior, but that would not make it human. It may converse intelligibly with other humans (ELIZA), it may learn from mistakes (Deep Blue), and it may make logical inferences that seem like real understanding (Watson). It is not hard to imagine an artificial intelligence that may even seem to have genuine feelings. It can be done with a sophisticated algorithm capable of analyzing human interactions and responding with the appropriate words to simulate a variety of emotions such as hate, love, annoyance, or boredom. The program can be combined with a speech synthesizer that adds the proper tone and inflections to the words.

According to Searle, a machine like that would be impressive, but not human. It is lacking an internal process that humans (and animals according to him) have that makes us "conscious." We are more than just machines taking in data (*chokhmah*) and manipulating symbols (*binah*) to spit out an output. As a person I have an added component that makes me "I." That is the component that informs "me" that "I" am playing *Jeopardy!* "I" know that the answers were right or wrong, and "I" know that "I" won. I believe that this third component of intelligence, the part that Searle calls consciousness, is what Jewish tradition calls "*daat.*"

In addition to *chokhmah* and *binah*, *daat* is the third type of intelligence mentioned in the Bible. Rashi translates *daat* as "*ruach hakodesh*" which means the divine spirit.

In his book *Inner Space*, Rabbi Aryeh Kaplan shows how Jewish mystical literature deals extensively with parsing the nuances of different forms of intelligence. It is quite astonishing that the ancients understood the relevance and importance of identifying distilled, distinct human intelligence thousands of years before computer technology would make it a practical study.

According to Jewish mysticism the highest form of intelligence, above *chokhmah* and *binah*, is represented by the term "*keter*," meaning crown. *Daat* is often used as an alternative term for *keter*; *keter* refers to the essence of the ineffable divine intelligence and *daat* is used when we are speaking of human intelligence.

Daat is qualitatively different from the other forms of intelligence that we have dealt with until now. In Rabbi Adin Steinsaltz's commentary to the authoritative Kabbalistic work *Tanya* he explains, "Without *daat*, there can be no realization of the person's…full structure of mental and emotional attributes. A person might have highly potent faculties of *chokhmah* and *binah*, but a lack of *daat* would prevent him from applying these powers to the direction and development of his own personality. So although *daat* does not add anything to a person's perception and understanding, its importance to the integrity of the soul's inner life is decisive. *Chokhmah* and *binah* are ways of gathering and processing data, but it is *daat* that creates the ability to produce an emotion. *Daat* is not an attribute in the way that *chokhmah* and *binah* are, rather *daat* is the force through which we acquire and process them. It is the faculty to reach conclusions based on the other forms of intelligence, it is the soul's connection to the subject, the part of the mind that decides 'This relates to me,' 'This is important to me.'"

Consciousness or *daat* is something that exists in even the simplest of living creatures. Even plants, according to the nineteenth century physician and botanist Dr. William Lauder Lindsay, have something like a "mind as it occurs in men." Daniel Chamovitz wrote in his book, *What a Plant Knows*, that plants are acutely "aware" of the world around them. They are aware of colors, of aromas, and of when they are being physically touched. To date, despite the impressive computers that can detect, analyze, and distinguish different sensations, to our knowledge these computers are not "aware" that these sensations are taking place.

Recently a group of roboticists devised a test to prove that a robot can have self-awareness. It is a variation of an old induction riddle called the King's Wise Man Test.

The original induction puzzle goes as follows: The King called the three wisest men in the country to his court to decide who would become his new advisor. He placed a hat on each of their heads, such that each wise man could see all of the other hats, but none of them could see his own. Each hat was either white or blue. The king gave his word to the wise men that at least one of them was wearing a blue hat – in other words, there could be one, two, or three blue hats, but not zero. The king also announced that the contest would be fair to all three men. The wise men were forbidden to speak to each other. The king declared that whichever man stood up first and announced the color of his own hat would become his new advisor.

The solution to the riddle can be found by looking at the hats of the other two advisors and based on the king's condition that the test is fair (i.e. all of the wise men will see the same thing when they look at the other two), and that all of the men are sufficiently wise (i.e. if any one of the men looked and saw two white hats he would be able to deduce that he was wearing the one blue hat), the truly wise man can deduce that all three must be wearing blue hats.

A group of roboticists at the Ransselaer Polytechnic Institute in New York built a trio of robots, two of which were given a dumbing pill that prevented them from talking, and the third was given an identical pill that was really a placebo. All three robots were asked to guess which robot was still able to speak. All attempted to say: "I don't know," and only one of them succeeded. When the robot heard its own voice say "I don't know," it immediately said, "Sorry, I know now! I was able to prove that I was not given a dumbing pill."

These robots merely passed a test of self-awareness, which is not an actual measure of self-awareness. They were programmed with a very impressive algorithm that used deductive reasoning. The test was clever, but not persuasive.

With enough ingenuity, an algorithm can be written to simulate any human experience. The challenge that is persistently posed to Searle's Chinese room argument is, given that a computer can demonstrate behavior that is indistinguishable to that of a human, how can you tell if consciousness is present or absent? Self-awareness and consciousness are by definition subjective experiences, so if a robot claims to be self-aware, there may be no way to objectively prove the claim one way or the other.

Free Will, Common Sense, and Morality

Another possible manifestation of *daat* is the ability to make moral conclusions based on the acquisition of other information. In the words of Rabbi Steinsaltz, "*Chokhmah* and *Binah* do not generate any definitive deductions, only an awareness. This is where the pivotal attribute of *daat* comes in: *daat* is the capacity to reach a conclusion, to impart an intellectual and moral bottom line to the abstract and undefinitive ideas of *chokhmah* and *binah*." In other words, *daat* represents our free will.

Determinists like B.F. Skinner believe that we may feel as though we have free choice, but in reality that feeling is an illusion. In his book *The End of Faith: Religion, Terror, and the Future of Reason*, atheist Sam Harris wrote, "In physical terms every action is clearly reducible to a totality of impersonal events merely propagating its influence: genes are transcribed, neurotransmitters bind to their receptors, muscle fibers contract, and John Doe pulls the trigger on his gun." We may think we have free will, but everything is predetermined by our genes. Some religious believers are in agreement with atheists on the point of determinism, they only disagree on what the determinant is, God or genetics.

To simultaneously believe in the God of the Bible and free will presents a contradiction. Either God is all powerful, or we have free will. Either God directs the course of history, or we determine our own destiny. The Talmud acknowledges and embraces the contradiction declaring, "Everything is foreseen, but freedom of choice is given."

Maimonides elaborates on this statement in his treatise on the laws of repentance.

"Free will is granted to all men. If one desires to turn himself to the path of good and be righteous, the choice is his. Should he desire to turn to the path of evil and be wicked, the choice is his...A person should not entertain the thesis held by the fools among the Gentiles and the majority of the undeveloped among Israel that, at the time of a man's creation, The Holy One, blessed be He, decrees whether he will be righteous or wicked. This is untrue. Each person is fit to be righteous like Moses, our teacher, or wicked, like Jeroboam. [Similarly,] he may be wise or foolish, merciful or cruel, miserly or generous, or [acquire] any other character traits. There is no one who compels him, sentences him, or leads him towards either of these two paths. Rather, he, on his own initiative and decision, tends to the path he chooses...This principle is a fundamental concept and a pillar [on which rests the totality] of the Torah. "

If God did not grant us free will and all of our actions were predetermined it would undermine the fundamental concept of reward and punishment. How could we be rewarded or punished for actions that were not really in our control?

After emphatically asserting the notion of free will, Maimonides sought to resolve the contradiction between free will and divine omniscience.

"One must know that everything is done in accord with His will and, nevertheless, we are responsible for our deeds. How is this [apparent contradiction] resolved?...Human knowledge cannot comprehend this concept in its entirety. Just as it is beyond the potential of man to comprehend and conceive the essential nature of the Creator, we do not have the potential to conceive how The Holy One, blessed be He, knows all the creations and their deeds. However, this is known without any doubt: man's actions are in his own hands and The Holy One, blessed be He, does not lead him [in a particular direction] or decree that he do anything."

According to Maimonides, our actions may be predetermined, but since we can't understand how God exercises his control on our fate, we are the ones who are in control of our choices. It seems to us that we have free will, so therefore we have free will. Similarly, philosopher Daniel Dennett, in his book *Elbow Room: The Varieties of Free Will Worth Wanting*, regards a person to have free will if his actions are determined by his internal decision processes, even if these processes themselves are deterministic. Maimonides' belief can be characterized as a form of compatibilism; the belief that free will and determinism are compatible ideas.

Taking a compatibilist view, computer scientist John McCarthy wrote a mathematical proof demonstrating that machines can have free will. His objective was not to make a philosophical point or to "console those who find determinism distressing," it was to "study which aspects of free will would make robots more useful."

McCarthy believes that free will is not all or nothing, there is a spectrum. A car, for instance, has no free will. It moves exactly as the operator directs it to move. A chess program like Deep Blue has some free will. On its own it makes "choices" about its next move. It does so by looking at all of the possible moves and ranking each one's chance of success based upon stored information about past games and a predetermined algorithm. Deep Blue makes a numerical calculation, and based on its analysis the program "chooses" its next move.

Humans don't have the time or the storage to make all of those calculations, so we make decisions based on the specific consequences of each action, rather than its statistical probability. In theory, a computer with considerably less computational power than Deep Blue could be programmed to play just as well as Deep Blue if it were given a more elaborate choice structure. For instance, certain positions could be rated as viable without giving precise numerical values. A move that advanced closer to one of those positions would be more preferable than one that did not. With this broader and less specific choice structure, the program may sometimes consider two or more options to be equally viable and may "choose" either one, as opposed to Deep Blue that will always choose the single option with the highest statistical probability of success.

Deep Blue makes choices on its own based on its strict algorithm. That is one type of free will. The more human-like chess program has a higher level of free will. It has to make a choice with less rigid parameters, a choice that is not objective. We might even call it "subjective." This distinction is the difference between just having "choice" and having "consciousness of choice." Creating consciousness of choice in a machine can be done, it just requires a more sophisticated and elaborate algorithm.

McCarthy's conclusion is that computers can have conscious free will, and his practical definition of conscious free will is an internal representation of the knowledge that ``I can, but I won't" and to behave accordingly.

Deep Blue is compelled to execute the one move that its algorithm has determined has the highest probability of success. It *can* only execute the move that it determines is the best move, and as long as it is able to execute it, Deep Blue must do so and *cannot* say I *won't*. A computer or robot with the ability to say, "*I can, but I won't*," demonstrates conscious free will. This is useful for making robots that are programmed for more complicated tasks that require common sense. Sometimes the immediate action that seems "correct" may not be the best course of action towards the completion of a broader more complicated goal.

Amelia Bedelia was the title character in a series of popular children's books about a housekeeper who had a tendency to misinterpret the written list of commands left by her employer by taking figures of speech and common terminology literally. When she was instructed to "Put the lights out," she took all of the light bulbs out of their sockets and hung them on a clothesline outside. When she was instructed to "Dust the furniture," she threw dusting powder all over the furniture. When she was told to "Dress the chicken," she put clothes on the chicken. When she was told to "Draw the drapes," she drew a picture of the drapes. Right before the performance of each task, Amelia Bedelia would always ask herself, "Why would my employer want me to do such a nonsensical thing?" Then she would remind herself that her employer had given strict instructions to do as the list told her, so she would do it.

A computer with no choice, or with unconscious choice, must stick to the strict instructions of its algorithm. A more sophisticated computer would recognize if certain instructions seem nonsensical or counterproductive towards a larger objective. It would have the choice to override its programming, decide that it *can but won't* follow the given directions, and figure out another way to follow the instructions in the manner that the human programmer intended. We call this kind of thinking common sense. That is what John McCarthy thought was one path to human level artificial intelligence; "to use mathematical logic to formalize common-sense knowledge in such a way that common-sense problems can be solved by logical reasoning."

McCarthy's monumental argument may also answer the question of whether a robot can be moral. "What exactly is morality?" is one of the fundamental questions of Jewish ethics, as articulated by Rabbi Basil Herring in his book *Jewish Ethics and Halakhah for Our Time*. Halakhah is an all-encompassing corpus of ritual and civil law derived from scripture and oral Jewish tradition. Rabbi Herring begins his study of ethics by asking the question, "To be a truly ethical person in practice, is it sufficient to follow the dictates of the *Halakhah* as formulated by halakhic authorities, or is it necessary in addition to subscribe to purely voluntary ethical principles that are a matter of personal conscience?" Is following the letter of the law sufficient, or is there a spirit of the law that stands above the code, and is in fact the true ends to which the Halakhah is only a means?

Rabbi A. I. Karelitz, known as Hazon Ish, in his book *Faith and Trust* wrote, "Punctilious observance of the law is the only path to the perfection of moral virtue." This seems to imply that all ethical positions must find justification in some legally binding Jewish rule or opinion. According to this view an intelligent computer could be perfectly moral by simply following the strict directives of the halakhic authorities in all cases.

Herring also cites an opposing view that "does not pretend to legislate rules to cover every situation, especially in those areas where so much depends on particular circumstances or conflicting principles...it leaves mundane and existential choices to man's reasoned decision, based on man's own moral sense of right and wrong."

In support of this view former Chief Rabbi of Israel A.I. Kook wrote in his *Orot Hatorah*, "Morality, in its naturalness, in all the depths of its splendor and power of its strength, must be determined in the soul...If we deafen our ears so that we cannot hear the simple call of the Lord which is potentially proclaimed through all the natural gates of light, which are in every man's reach, because we think that we will find the light of the Torah in a Torah which is severed from all the light of life spread over the world and planted in the splendid soul of man, then we have not understood the value of the Torah."

Rabbi Kook and others believe that morality is more than a list of rules that oblige a specific action (positive law), rather it is an inherently rational system (natural law). The ability to override a given order, to follow a conscience, comes from our soul. McCarthy believes that a computer can be programmed with common sense necessary to complete a complicated task. One wonders if Rabbi Kook would consider a robot programmed with a broad and sophisticated algorithm that gave it the ability to abstain from instructions that it "sensed" were "wrong" as having a soul. Would such a robot be considered a moral robot with a conscience?

Common sense programming will undoubtedly make better robots that will be more helpful in more situations, but it will not make them human. The free will that makes someone truly human, not artificially so, is more than just the ability to use common sense to accomplish a task. It's not only *"I can, but I won't,"* it's also *"I shouldn't, but I will."* One of the things that currently separate us from machines is that we can not only abstain from an action that is permitted, but we can also consciously commit an act that we know to be harmful or to be morally wrong. Humans can sin.

Robots do what they are programmed to do. Dr. Susan Calvin, from Isaac Asimov's *I Robot* points out that there is a world of difference between robots and men. "Robots are essentially decent." In one of the stories the characters are having a difficult time determining if a certain person is a man or really a robot. Although the person has the appearance of a man, he seems to conform to all of the rules of robotics. Dr. Calvin points out, "Actions such as his could come only from a robot, or from a very honorable and decent human being. But you see, you just can't differentiate between a robot and the very best of humans."

A robot can be programmed to lie, cheat, steal, and even kill, but that does not make it an evil robot. That is a robot doing exactly what some human programmed it to do. An evil robot would be one that knows that it should not lie, cheat, steal, and kill, yet decides to do it anyway, just like a human.

There are evil people capable of making robots that cause harm, but currently we do not have robots that are capable of being evil on their own. Let us imagine that one day it would be possible to create a robot that can decide to disregard its programming for good and commit acts of evil. We need to ask ourselves, why would we want such a robot?

Teiku

John McCarthy wrote a paper arguing that robots should not be programmed with human intelligence. Among his arguments he writes "It is also practically important to avoid making robots that are reasonable targets for either human sympathy or dislike. If robots are visibly sad, bored or angry, humans, starting with children, will react to them as persons. Then they would very likely come to occupy some status in human society. Human society is complicated enough already."

The question really is not could we make such a robot, but should we make such a robot. What utility would such a robot have?

In the Biblical story of the Garden of Eden, Adam and Eve became mortal when they ate from the Tree of Knowledge of Good and Bad. "Knowledge of Good and Bad" is what makes us human, whether it means the capacity to choose good over evil, or the manic depressive state we experience while contemplating whether life is beautiful or meaningless. Whatever it means, it is what makes us unique among all of God's creatures, and the consequence of its acquisition is banishment from paradise. Ignorance is bliss.

The human experience is complex and tortuous. We are anxious, self-conscious, depressed, we are riddled with contradictions and self-doubt. We are in a constant pursuit of happiness that seems perpetually elusive. We are challenged with temptation and often fail, we fall short of living up to our ideals, and we rarely live out our dreams. We throw our hands up in despair asking ourselves, "What does it all mean?" "Why are we here?" "What is the point?" And after all that we die.

The Talmud teaches that in the end of days both the righteous and the wicked will look back on their lives and weep. The wicked will weep from a sense of immense regret for the bad choices they made, and the righteous will weep when they recall the suffering they endured in order to do what was right in the face of adversity. Life is hard, unfair, and ridden with anguish. The Talmud also recounts a long standing argument over whether or not man would have been better off if he were never created. In the end, the consensus was that given the choice we would have been better off if man had never been created. If that is what it means to be human, to program a robot with a soul would be nothing short of cruelty.

We must then ask, why do we bother creating any new souls? How do we justify bringing children into this world filled with suffering? This is an especially difficult question for someone who believes that we are just a pack of neurons leading random and purposeless lives. Indeed, according to a number of studies including those done by the Pew Research Center, on average atheists have fewer children than religious people. I will not attempt to answer for the atheist.

The question is no less difficult for the believer in God and the divine soul. Here, dear reader, I must admit, I have no answer. I do not profess to know the meaning of life. However, the Bible tells us where to search for it.

The end of the story about the Garden of Eden tells us that there is an antidote, a path back to Eden, a way to possess knowledge of good and bad and still reside in paradise.

"And the Lord God said, 'Behold Man has become like the Unique One among us, knowing good and bad; and now lest he put forth his hand and take also of the Tree of Life, and eat and live forever.'"

Hidden behind the cherubs tasked with guarding the path is the Tree of Life. In the book of Proverbs the Torah itself is referred to as the "Tree of Life," and when the children of Israel traveled in the wilderness the Torah resided in the Ark of the Covenant, also guarded by the cherubim. This is no coincidence. The lesson is that somehow the meaning of life is found in the study and the observance of Torah.

So we come to the end of the line. The Talmud has a word that designates an argument as immutable, unanswerable based on the available information. The word is *teiku*. In Modern Hebrew *teiku* means a tie or a draw. Perhaps one day it will be possible to program a robot with truly human level intelligence, or even with a human soul. I am personally skeptical, but I am open to the idea that it is possible. Nobody knows for sure. The question remains a teiku.

One thing is clear. As new technologies are developed, at all times it is imperative that we stay on the path guarded by the cherubim, the path towards the Tree of Life. We cannot allow technology to confuse us and lead us astray, off of the path of life. Technology can and must be used as a tool and a vehicle to bring us closer to Eden.

9: Tainted Grain

Simple Lifers

In 1985 there were 300,000 cell phones subscribers in the United States. By 2010 there were over 300 million. That's almost everyone. At one time only wealthy people had them. Today only eccentrics do not. Individuals or communities that attempt to conspicuously avoid certain technologies are subject to ridicule and scorn, and are increasingly inconvenienced and disadvantaged as more and more aspects of our regular home and work routines become mechanized, automated, and digitized.

Even if it were possible to opt out, why would we want to deliberately deprive ourselves of the conveniences and benefits of technologies that improve the quality of our lives? In some cases it is considered morally questionable, if not outright immoral, to opt out. It is not hard to imagine a not-so-distant future in which depriving children of the educational, protective, and life enhancing services provided by robots would be looked upon as raising children without teaching them to read. Worse, it may be viewed as people who refuse organ transplants, blood transfusions, or vaccines.

As intelligent robots become more pervasive and we increasingly depend upon them in our daily lives, it will no longer be a choice as to whether or not to use them. They will be here and, like cell phones, we won't even remember how we ever got along without them.

Futurists anticipate that anti-robot movements will develop. In Isaac Asimov's fictional future they are known as the Fundamentalists. "They were not a political party; they made pretense to no formal religion. Essentially they were those who had not adapted themselves to what had once been called the Atomic Age, in the days when atoms were a novelty. Actually, they were the Simple-Lifers, hungering after a life, which to those who lived it had probably appeared not so simple, and who had been, therefore, Simple-Lifers themselves."

In the early 1800s in the English Midlands bands of weavers and knitters rose up in rebellion against the big textile mills and factories that threatened to destroy their cottage industry and make their jobs obsolete. The rebels called themselves Luddites, after a worker named Ned Ludlam who, according to legend, smashed the technological idols of his master.

Today a Luddite is a derogatory term used to describe anyone who is opposed to technological progress. Extreme opposition to emerging technologies, especially lifesaving technologies, is not only an act of self-immolation; it is an exercise in futility. Anti-movements are rarely successful.

Richard Nixon is reported to have said, "If you ever hear of a group forming to stop X, put your money on X."

Technovolatility

In a lecture at the Singularity Summit in 2010, futurist Eliezer Yudkowsky described different attitudes towards technology. A technophile thinks technology is all good. A technophobe thinks all technology is bad. Someone who is technonormal believes "All this talk of golden ages and planet wide catastrophes is childish, life will go on."

Rabbi Avigdor Miller was a technonormalist. When asked in 1973 about whether the new Space Age contradicted the Biblical statement "There is nothing new under the sun," Rabbi Miller answered, "No. All Mankind's interests continue the same. God, life, death, earning a livelihood, pleasures, human relations, and tests of virtue."

Rabbi Miller's approach is predicated on a fundamental belief that the world is run by God, and that history is moving along according to a divine plan towards a preordained destiny. The Jewish belief in the Messiah is the optimistic belief that ultimately the world will be redeemed and we will emerge from all of our suffering into an epoch of peace and prosperity. At that time suffering of any kind will be eradicated and humanity will reach its full potential.

This is oddly similar to the messianic predictions of Ray Kurzweil and the cult of the Singularity. They believe that in a not so distant future people will merge with machines. Super intelligent robots will rid the world of war, disease, and any inefficiencies that cause discord and suffering.

Yudkowsky is not so optimistic. He classifies himself as technovolatile. He believes that "The future might be extremely good or extremely bad, but it isn't likely to end up anywhere in between." He does not believe that there is any guarantee that people will never create technologies that will eventually destroy humanity, nor does he believe that technology will inevitably be a force of good in the world.

In his book *The Net Delusion*, Evgeny Morosov reminds us that every time a new form of technology emerges that fundamentally changes the world people have a tendency to think that we have reached Utopia. In 1858 an editorial proclaimed, "The telegraph binds together by a vital cord all the nations of the earth…It is impossible that old prejudices and hostilities should longer exist, while such an instrument has been created for an exchange of thought between all the nations of earth."

In the 1930s the airplane was expected to "foster democracy, equality, and freedom, to purge the world of war and violence; even give rise to a new kind of human being." The radio was supposed to "make war impossible, because it will make war ridiculous." Television was supposed to disband armies and create a whole new democratic world in ways never before imagined."

Morosov notes that "The rhetoric that accompanied predictions about earlier technologies was usually every bit as sublime as today's quasi-religious discourse about the internet."

Technovolatile means that the future is unwritten. New technologies do not set the inevitable course of human history. Humanity sets its own course and creates its own destiny.

Two thousand years ago, two of the leading sages of the Talmud had a conversation that could have taken place today. The Roman Empire at the time was not friendly towards the Jewish People. Rome had conquered Israel, destroyed the Temple, and quashed any semblance of Jewish resistance in Israel in the rebellion of Bar Kochvah. Nevertheless, Rabbi Yehudah extolled the virtues of Rome's political, economic, and technological developments. He pointed to their market places that made commerce more accessible, the bridges that facilitate easier transportation, and the bathhouses that provided advanced medical care. His colleague Rabbi Shimon was not as impressed. He maintained that Roman progress was motivated by selfishness, lust, and greed. The market places were for prostitutes, the bridges were for the collection of tolls, and the bathhouses were for pampering and vanity.

If the conversation were to take place today, Rabbi Shimon would probably point out that our online marketplace was pioneered by purveyors of pornography, the bridges of fiber optic cables that carry our information at lightning speed were developed so that Wall Street firms could exploit and manipulate markets, and some of the far-reaching medical advances that some futurists talk about seem to be less about healing and more about living out sexual fantasies and fetishes.

Rabbi Yehudah and Rabbi Shimon were not arguing over the genius of Roman technologies. Both were, no doubt, impressed by these incredible achievements. Nor were they arguing over whether the Romans were a degenerate and wicked culture. In that they were in full agreement. Rabbi Yehudah, however, felt that we can look past the motivations behind the inventions and simply appreciate them for the benefits that they bring to the world. Rabbi Shimon felt that we cannot ignore the motivations, because he believed that technologies developed for the purpose of evil will eventually be used for evil, not for good.

The prophet Isaiah said, "Should you glorify the ax over the one who cuts with it?" In modern parlance, guns don't kill people, people kill people. Good technologies in the hands of bad people can and will cause harm to innocent people. The people don't even have to be bad, just careless. Often technological solutions solve one problem while creating a whole new set of problems that were unimagined before, often worse than the problem that we were solving. Morosov points out that cars were supposed to make the environment cleaner than horses. The industrial revolution made life easier, but now we fear that its byproducts may destroy the planet.

While certain beneficial technologies can be misused, others are created as inherently harmful. Computer viruses, nuclear weapons, and sexbots can potentially be used for good, but their functions are nefarious and destructive by design. Our course is not determined by our inventions, but by how we develop and use them. Technology is a vehicle. The direction that it takes depends on the intentions of the driver.

Cain's Legacy

The fourth chapter of Genesis is a collection of short episodes about the descendants of history's first murderer, Cain, the son of Adam. Some of Cain's progeny were incredibly adept at developing new technologies. Enoch was the first builder, Jabal was the first to domesticate animals, and Jubal was the first musician. Tubal-Cain was the first to forge tools of copper and iron. According to the commentator Rashi, tubal means to "improve by adding spices." He was given the name because he used his metallurgical gifts to create weapons and "spice up the craft of his ancestor Cain the Murderer."

Jewish tradition says that the wicked behavior of these generations caused the great flood to come and destroy the earth. Their technology enabled them to conquer nature and free them from the curse of Adam that sentenced them to earn their bread by the sweat of their brow, but instead of using their newly found leisure time to develop their values, they occupied themselves with acts of debauchery that lead to moral decline.

The Bible contrasts the legacy of Cain with that of his brother Seth. Seth was righteous and produced a descendant named Noah. Noah was obviously technologically savvy, as the ark that he built proved capable of withstanding the greatest natural disaster in history. Cain's descendants were most likely equally capable of constructing an ark. It was not Noah's ingenuity that saved him, it was his morality.

Evgeny Morosov wrote, "For [technology] to play a constructive role in ridding the world of prejudice and hatred, it needs to be accompanied by an extremely ambitious set of social and political reforms; in their absence social ills may only get worse." Technology alone cannot save the world; our technology must be rooted in moral values.

Technology allows us to relax our physical muscles, but requires us to strengthen our values. The more advanced the technology the more important it is to study and develop our understanding of the nuances of morality and ethics. Artificial intelligence will present moral challenges as great as any technology that came before it. We can't know all of the consequences that may come from it, but neither are we free from trying to anticipate them. Now more than ever we need thoughtful leaders who are equipped to understand these challenges, to articulate their nature, and to offer alternatives and solutions to problematic innovations. We must be courageous in the face of large corporations who may be tempted by profits to release technologies that could be harmful to everyone.

We are entering a brave new world. Sooner than we think we will be surrounded by these new machines, they will become an integral part of our lives. It will become increasingly harder remind ourselves what life was like before them, and to maintain certain values that will seem obsolete.

Rabbi Nachman of Breslav told a story called *The Tainted Grain*. The king's star gazer saw that the grain harvested that year was tainted. Anyone who would eat from it would become insane. "What can we do?" said the king. "It is not possible to destroy the crop for we do not have enough grain stored to feed the entire population."

"Perhaps," said the star gazer, "we should set aside enough grain for ourselves. At least that way we could maintain our sanity." The king replied, "If we do that, we'll be considered crazy. If everyone behaves one way and we behave differently, we'll be considered the not normal ones."

"Rather," said the king, "I suggest that we too eat from the crop, like everyone else. However, to remind ourselves that we are not normal, we will make a mark on our foreheads. Even if we are insane, whenever we look at each other, we will remember that we are insane."

All of us who want to preserve morality in the new world must constantly remind each other of the importance of doing so. We must be courageous and resolute in the face of the brave new world, and remind each other that we are not alone. Not because, as Asimov wrote, we will have robots, but because we have our fellow man.

Acknowledgements

This book was inspired by my friend and teacher, Moshe Goldfeder, who introduced me to the topic of robots and continues to encourage and inspire me.

I do not have expertise in any of the specialties that a comprehensive study on this topic requires. I am indebted to the experts whose works educated and informed me. I was particularly influenced by Evgeny Morosov, Jaron Lanier, and the late John McCarthy.

This book could not have been written without the assistance of internet search engines. Resources that once would take weeks and months to find were available to me in seconds. I also want to thank the many anonymous authors on Wikipedia who pointed me to sources that I otherwise never would have found. I wish that I could thank them by name.

Ray Kurzweil's inventions have changed the world and bettered the lives of countless people, nevertheless, I humbly submit that some of his philosophical ideas are wrong. If my tone seems forceful it is because the stakes are high, but no disrespect is intended. I have no doubt that his intentions are pure and that he is driven by a search for truth, no less than I am.

Thank you to my classes at Beth Tfiloh, my Monday morning adult education class and my 8th grade Talmud class, for helping me develop my thoughts.

Thank you to all of those who read the manuscript and gave me feedback: Ed Schlesinger, Yoni Bedine, Avi Benus, Ron Gartenhaus, Yitz Jacob, Frank Pipesh, Marvin Rombro, Lee Vogelstein, and my parents David and Sandy Gross.

Thank you to Eli and Mila Burman for your encouragement, support, inspiration, and friendship.

Special thanks to my editors, Melvin Lessing and Deborah Vogelstein; their superb editing was a gift for which I will be forever grateful. I take full responsibility for errors, including grammar and spelling. Thanks to my layout designers Joel and Rachel Greene from Penoaks Publishing for their excellent work, and to Serena Cohen and Fraydee Mozes for help with my cover design.

This book was written for my children. I hope and pray that they grow to love and cherish the Torah, and to recognize the importance of perpetuating the immutable values of the Torah in an ever-changing world.

Finally, I want to thank my wife, Miriam, the true coauthor of this book, and partner in everything I do. No robot could ever replace you.

Bibliography

Asimov, Isaac. *Asimov's Guide to the Bible: The Old Testament, Vol 1.* New York: Avon, 1971.

Asimov, Isaac. *I, Robot.* New York: Bantam, 1950.

Asimov, Isaac. *Robot Dreams.* New York: Berkley, 1986.

Barrat, James. *Our Final Invention: Artificial Intelligence and the End of the Human Era.* New York: St. Martin, 2013.

Bleich, J. David. "Vegetarianism and Judaism." *Tradition: A Journal of Orthodox Jewish Thought* 23(1) (Summer 1987): 82-90. Print.

Bleich, J. David. *With Perfect Faith: The Foundations of Jewish Belief.* New York: Ktav, 1983.

Broyde, Michael J. "Cloning People and Jewish Law: A Preliminary Analysis." *Journal of Halacha and Contemporary Society* 34 (Fall 1997): 27-65. Print.

Carr, Nicholas. *The Glass Cage: How Our Computers Are Changing Us.* New York: Norton, 2014.

Carr, Nicholas. *The Shallows: What the Internet is Doing to Our Brains.* New York: Norton, 2011.

Chamovitz, Daniel. *What a Plant Knows: A Field Guide to the Senses.* New York: Farrar, Straus and Giroux, 2013.

Cohen, Jared and Eric Schmidt. *The New Digital Age: Transforming Nations, Businesses, and Our Lives.* New York: Vintage, 2014.

Crick, Francis. *The Astonishing Hypothesis: The Scientific Search for the Soul.* New York: Scribner, 1995.

Dennett, Daniel. *Elbow Room: The Varieties of Free Will Worth Wanting.* Cambridge: MIT, 1984.

Dershowitz, Alan. *America on Trial: Inside the Legal Battles that Transformed our Nation.* New York: Grand Central, 2005.

Dershowitz, Alan. *Rights from Wrongs: The Origins of Human Rights in the Experience of Injustice.* New York: Basic, 2004

Durkheim, Emile. "The Idea of the Soul." *The Elementary Forms of the Religious Life.* New York: Free Press, 1965.

Goldfeder, Mark. "Not All Dogs Go to Heaven: Judaism's Lessons in Beastly Morality." *Animal Law Review* 20(1) (Spring 2014). Web.

Goldfeder, Mark and Yosef Razin. "Robotic Marriage and the Law." *LSD Journal* Vol. 10 (2015): 137-176. Web.

Guizzo, Erico. "Hiroshi Ishiguro: The Man Who Made a Copy of Himself." *IEEE Spectrum.* 23 April 2010. Web.

Harris, Sam. *The End of Faith: Religion, Terror, and the Future of Reason.* New York: Norton, 2005.

Herring, Basil F. *Jewish Ethics and Halakhah for Our Time: Sources and Commentary.* New York: Ktav, 1984.

Hitchens, Christopher. *God is Not Great: How Religion Poisons Everything.* New York: Twelve, 2007.

Holiday, Ryan. *Trust Me I'm Lying: Confessions of a Media Manipulator.* New York: Portfolio, 2013.

Hunter, George W. "Scopes Trial - Excerpts from Hunter's Civic Biology." *Famous Trials by Douglas O. Linder: UMKC School of Law.* 24 June 2013. Web.

Idel, Moshe. *Golem: Jewish Magical and Mystical Traditions on the Artificial Anthropoid.* New York: State Univ. of New York, 1989.

Johnson, Harriet McBryde. "Unspeakable Conversations." *New York Times Magazine.* 16 February 2003. Web.

Jones, Richard. "Against Transhumanism: The Delusion of Technological Transcendence." *Softmachines.* 15 January 2016. E-book.

Kaplan, Aryeh. *Encounters.* New York: Moznaim, 1990.

Kaplan, Aryeh. *Inner Space: Introduction to Kabbalah, Meditation, and Prophecy.* New York: Moznaim, 1991.

Kaplan, Aryeh. *Rabbi Nachman's Stories.* New York: Breslov Research Institute, 1985.

Kaplan, Aryeh. *Sefer Yetzirah The Book of Creation: In Theory and Practice.* York Beach: Samuel Weiser, 1990.

Kripke, Saul. *Naming and Necessity.* Cambridge: Harvard, 1972.

Kurzweil, Ray. *The Age of Spiritual Machines: When Computers Exceed Human Intelligence.* New York: Penguin, 1999.

Kurzweil, Ray. *The Singularity is Near: When Humans Transcend Biology.* New York: Penguin, 2005.

LaBoissiere, Michael. *Sexbots, Killbots, and Virtual Dogs: Essays on Ethics and Technology.* Dr. Michael C. Labossiere, 2014.

Lanier, Jaron. *Who Owns The Future?* New York: Simon and Schuster, 2013.

Lanier, Jaron. *You Are Not a Gadget: A Manifesto.* New York: Vintage, 2010.

Levy, Steven. *In the Plex: How Google Thinks, Works, and Shapes Our Lives.* New York: Simon and Schuster, 2011.

Luzzatto, Moshe C. *Way of God: Derech Hashem.* Trans. Aryeh Kaplan. New York: Feldheim, 1981.

Maimonides. *Mishnah Torah: The Laws of Repentance*. Trans. Eliyahu Touger. Chabad-Lubavitch Media Center. Web.

McCarthy, John. "Free Will-Even for Robots." *Formal Reasoning Group: John McCarthy's Home Page*. 21 November 1999. Web.

McCarthy, John. "John Searle's Chinese Room Argument." *Formal Reasoning Group: John McCarthy's Home Page*. 21 September 2001. Web.

McCarthy, John. "Programs with Common Sense." *Formal Reasoning Group: John McCarthy's Home Page*. 1 March 2003. Web.

McCarthy, John. "The Robot and the Baby." *Formal Reasoning Group: John McCarthy's Home Page*. 16 October 2004. Web.

McCarthy, John. "What is Artificial Intelligence?" *Formal Reasoning Group: John McCarthy's Home Page*. 12 November 2007. Web.

Miller, Avigdor. *Sing You Righteous: A Jewish Seekers Ideology*. New York: Balshon, 1973.

Morosov, Evgeny. *The Net Delusion: The Dark Side of Internet Freedom*. New York: Public Affairs, 2011.

Morosov, Evgeny. *To Save Everything Click Here: The Folly of Technological Solutionsim*. New York: Public Affairs, 2013.

Myers, PZ. "Ray Kurzweil does not Understand the Brain." Web blog post. *Pharyngula*. ScienceBlogs.com. 17 August 2010. Web.

Nagel, Thomas. *Mind and Cosmos: Why the Materialist Neo Darwinian Conception of Nature is Almost Certainly False*. New York: Oxford, 2012.

Paglia, Camille. "Camille Paglia takes on Jon Stewart, Trump, Sanders: 'Liberals think of themselves as very open-minded, but that's simply not true!'" Interview by Dave Daley. *Salon.* 29 July 2015. Web.

Pinker, Steven. *The Stuff of Thought: Language as a Window into Human Nature.* New York: Penguin, 2008.

Platos Cave. William Lane Craig: *Materialistic Reductionism, Mind & Consciousness.* Online Video Clip. Youtube. 18 May 2013.

Raphall, Morris. J. "The Bible View of Slavery." *Jewish-American History Documentation Foundation.* 2016. Web.

Rosenes, Yaakov. "Ask Rabbi Google??!!" Web blog post. *The Seforim Blog.* 25 July 2014. Web.

Rosenfeld, Azriel. "Human Identity: Halakhic Issues." *Tradition: A Journal of Orthodox Jewish Thought* 16(3) (Spring 1977): 58-74. Print.

Rosenfeld, Azriel. "Religion and the Robot." *Tradition: A Journal of Orthodox Jewish Thought* 8(3) (Fall 1966): 15-26. Print.

Searle, John. "Watson Doesn't Know it Won 'Jeopardy!'" *The Wall Street Journal.* 23 February 2011. Web.

Scholem, Gershom. "The Golem of Prague and the Golem of Rehovoth." *Commentary.* 1 January 1966. Web.

Scholem, Gershom. *Kabbalah.* Jerusalem: Keter, 1974.

Scholem, Gershom. *On the Kabbalah and Its Symbolism.* New York: Schocken, 1965.

Shanahan, Murray. "Consciousness in Human-Level A.I." *What to Think About Machines That Think: Today's Leading Thinkers on the Age of Machine Intelligence.* Ed. John Brockman. New York: Harper, 2015.

Shirky, Clay. *Here Comes Everyone: The Power of Organizing Without Organizations.* New York: Penguin, 2009.

Singer, Peter. *Animal Liberation: A New Ethics for Our Treatment of Animals.* New York: Avon, 1975.

Singularity Videos. *Ray Kurzweil Interviews Prof. Alan Dershowitz - The Legal Rights of A.I.* Online Video Clip. Youtube. 15 January 2016.

Singularity Summit. *Eliezer Yudkowsky on Intelligence Explosion.* Online Video Clip. Youtube. 21 February 2012.

Soloveitchik, Joseph B. *Halakhic Man.* Trans. Lawrence Kaplan. Philadelphia: Jewish – Publication Society, 1983.

Soloveitchik, Joseph B. "The Lonely Man of Faith." *Tradition: A Journal of Orthodox Jewish Thought* 7(2) (Summer 1965): Print.

Steiner, Christopher. *Automate This: How Algorithms Took Over Markets, Our Jobs, and the World.* New York: Penguin, 2012.

Steinsaltz, Adin. *Opening the Tanya: Discovering the Moral and Mystical Teaching of a Classic Work of Kabbalah.* San Francisco: Jossey-Bass, 2003.

Surowieki, James. *The Wisdom of Crowds: Why the Many Are Smarter Than the Few and How Collective Wisdom Shapes Business, Economies, Societies and Nations.* . New York: Anchor, 2005.

Talks at Google. *John Searle: "Consciousness in Artificial Intelligence" Talks at Google.* Online Video Clip. Youtube. 3 December 2015.

Ted Talks. *Guy Hoffman: Robots with "Soul."* Online Video Clip. Youtube. 17 January 2014.

Vital, Chayyim. *The Tree of Life: The Place of Adam Kadmon - Chayyim Vital's Introduction to the Kabbalah of Isaac Luria.* Trans. Donald Wildern Menzi and Zwe Padeh. New York: Arizal, 1999.

Index

About the Author

Rabbi Jonathan Gross received his BA in mathematics from Yeshiva College and his rabbinic ordination from the Rabbi Isaac Elchanan Theological Seminary of Yeshiva University. He served as the Chief Rabbi of the State of Nebraska for 10 years, and most recently was a rabbi at Baltimore's Beth Tfiloh Congregation, one of the largest Orthodox Synagogues in North America. He is currently a student at the University of Baltimore School of Law.

Made in the USA
Charleston, SC
25 August 2016